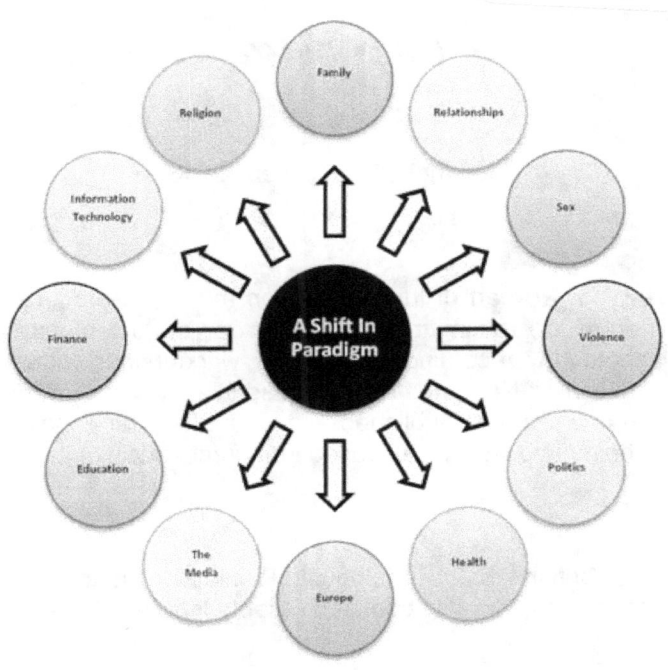

A Shift
In Paradigm

Exploring 21St Century Society

For Everyday People

J D Milaric

A Bright Pen Book

British Library Cataloguing Publication Data.
A catalogue record for this book is available from the British Library

ISBN 978-0-7552-1541-6

Authors OnLine Ltd
19 The Cinques
Gamlingay, Sandy
Bedfordshire SG19 3NU
England

This book is also available in e-book format,
details of which are available at www.authorsonline.co.uk

In honour of my mum and dad - the people who helped shape my life and my wife who has been an inspiration to me throughout our marriage not to mention our two sons who together with their wives have brought me into the 21st century.

CONTENTS

PROFILE OF THE AUTHOR

THE PREAMBLE

HOW TO ENGAGE WITH THIS BOOK

THE SUBJECT MATTER:-

1. OUR MONIES – FINANCE IN THESE MODERN TIMES
2. HOW WE BEHAVE – OUR LIFESTYLES
3. HEALTH AND PERSONAL MAINTENANCE – LOOKING AFTER OURSELVES
4. FAMILY – WHERE WE BELONG
5. THE STATE OF GOVERNMENT – TAKING CHARGE AND RESPONSIBILITY
6. RELIGION IN THIS AGE – HAVING FAITH
7. A ROLE FOR EACH PERSON – ROOTING THIS OUT
8. COMMUNICATIONS & THE MEDIA IN TODAY'S WORLD

POSTCRIPT – IT's YOUR CALL NOW

MY APPRECIATION OF OTHER PEOPLE INVOLVED

NOTES – ANSWERS

REFERENCES – MEANING AND THE SOURCES

PROFILE OF THE AUTHOR

I commenced this project just over 2 years ago in my early 50's which today might be termed middle-aged or possibly a bit "past it". In a discussion about how to use my time after ceasing work on medical grounds towards the end of 2010, my elder son suggested writing a book and I enquired of him about what? He replied "your wisdom and thoughts on life". Initially I questioned myself as to really being fit for this purpose having led an ordinary life working, bringing up a family together with my wife, undertaking voluntary work with some charities, been a Cub Scout Leader for a local pack and travelled to some different countries for holidays and business commitments.

I regard my time on this earth to date as a life well led but not exceptional or worthy of a literary composition. Then I had an "epiphany" which funnily enough is one of my elder son's favourite words. I do have a lot to say about what is happening in our world, enjoy in-depth and controversial discussions, have come across a lot of interesting individuals from many walks of life and always enjoyed face to face contact with people.

Precisely on account of having not scaled any particular heights in my profession or private life (with no complaints about this situation) but with a lot to say and time on my hands, this did seem to be right for me at this juncture. In a position now to reflect upon and put forward my views and resolutions on a wide range of issues that I am passionate about, as are many people who I have enjoyed being in contact with, I began to think more to the point why not do this? These thoughts traverse many disciplines – philosophy, social issues, economics, health, religion, politics, history, sport, entertainment, current affairs and the media. Hopefully the appeal of this book to a broad range of readers will be that it does not easily "fit into any particular category" or instantly attract comparison with an existing publication.

I worked in the financial services industry my whole life from age 18 until now – a period spanning 35 years, mostly as an IFA (Independent Financial Adviser), but over the recent years focusing on the provision of training to and assessment of people with regard to the industry required examinations. I was employed for some years during the earlier part of my career in managerial positions and then subsequently for a large number of years operated on a self-employed basis.

Outside of work, I have been involved with a number of charities to raise money and awareness of their activities including Norwood, the British Heart Foundation (BHF), Jewish Blind Society (as it was known in my teens) and Hope For Children (HOPE). I came across many dedicated people and whilst I will always extol the virtues of charitable undertakings, cannot escape feeling that in too many instances today, this replaces what should be provided by the State from our taxes and National Insurance Contributions (NIC). Charitable funds are intended to be supplemental to and not instead of appropriate state provision for children, the elderly and those vulnerable people in society.

Keeping fit and doing exercise has always been part of life for me since I was much younger and up until my late 40's, regularly going swimming, walking long distances, cycling extensively and participating in various charity and publicly organised cycle rides, whilst most recently I developed a penchant for running. Running in three Flora London Marathons was amongst my most memorable escapades (all of which were in the last few years) and whilst the finishing times were disappointing and I had to walk parts of the course with each one, the training and preparation were great incentives to eat better, allocate time for my marathon schedule and be part of something very special. One marathon I took part in together with my eldest son and another with both of my sons – great family experiences.   I came across so many wonderful people full of giving and positivity on marathon days and wished this could apply at all other times of the year during commuting, working and generally life itself.

I learned some valuable lessons consequent upon running the marathons which have been instrumental for me writing this book.   Most people are inherently good and capable of achieving great feats if they put their minds to it. There is no requirement for expensive equipment and participation in an event like this can change your perspective on life forever. The marathon experiences also taught me that a person of any age or background can become fitter, healthier and spiritually better off. No doubt this applies to many other similar charitable activities and sports.

My time as an Assistant Cub Scout Leader for over 14 years combined with all of the camping experiences involved had an impact on me both as an individual and father. Some children aged 8 to 10½ struggled with the outdoors, missed their home conveniences and games, did not know how to carry out some basic activities even at that age and generally were "more suited to an indoor world". But quite soon these boys and the overall majority wallowed in the freedom to run around, familiarise themselves about nature, get dirty without a parent's recrimination, learn how to use their time and play even in wet and windy weather, and perhaps most importantly learnt the art of sharing with others.

I believe that the scouting movement for both boys and girls is more apt today than ever before to help build our youngster's characters, appreciate the great outdoors and world around them as well as trying out new activities in a properly supervised environment. My youngest son loved his time in the cubs and scouts and I saw how he interacted with the other boys and nature to everybody's benefit. In these times when the trend is to spend more time in cars, playing various games inside the home, exercising and spending less and less time outdoors - being a bit independent and enjoying fresh air are important for our children. Good health and keeping fit can at least be instigated by involvement on the scouting movement or undertaking similar activities at an early age.

I am a practising Jew observant in some respects, but by no means strict or fully orthodox in my way of life. I enjoy being able to go about my religious activities without hindrance and being part of a large Jewish community whilst in my work and other aspects of life, feeling integrated into English society and proud of the country where I was born, brought up and live today. I respect and like many of our country's traditions and if I may say quirks that define England and what it represents to it's citizens and people around the world. Where we want to and do not feel this as some sort of outmoded way of living, following our religious heritage and having faith can enhance our lives and ensure that we are in tune with much of the modern way of living. For over 30 years (with hopefully many more to come) I have been fortunate to enjoy a very happy marriage to my wife – together we have shared raising our two sons and now also have grandchildren to delight in.

There are numerous jokes circulating about marriage as an institution, a life sentence and how men are not meant to be with the same woman all of their lives (you are probably recalling these right now) and of course we have laughed at them. A stable and enjoyable family life I ardently believe is the best possible basis for our children to learn about and develop their characters and preparation for when they "flee the nest". All families have their ups and downs but a loving husband and wife, mother and father can weather these and produce the best possible outcome – parents for the next generation.

I was made redundant twice during my working life, came across death at close quarters having lost my parents not long ago and recently was compelled to stop work due to ill-health. These are not only lifestyle events common to many people, but also "life defining" ones. The extent to which I possess any wisdom that is worthy of a book being written is for you to judge. Along with a lot of other individuals, I have endured good and bad times in my life and do not claim that these are in any sense unique. The notions put forward in the pages that follow are based upon experiences which I have endured in conjunction with my outlook on the future. I fervently believe that radical changes are essential for humankind and time may run out on many levels for us to take appropriate measures along the lines outlined in this book – to avoid **the bankruptcy of humanity.**

Join with me on a trek into my mind in the pages which follow, if you have anything to say about how you live and the world around us. The book embodies the stance of an ordinary person living in England in 2013 who is not and has no aspirations to be a politician, celebrity of any kind or change the world single-handed. A particular feature of and intention in writing the book is to adopt a non-political stance regarding the issues covered and any solutions put forward, we are in dire need of a new kind of **manifesto for life.**

At this juncture, try to discard notions of being religious or not, left or right wing or in the centre with your views, liberal, socialist, green, academic, practical, a high earner, on a perceived low income or currently out of work, single parent, married or in a relationship, able-bodied or not in good health or any other criterion for individuals that I have missed out and you deem appropriate for yourself. This publication aims to transcends such labels – essential if a positive outcome is to be achieved. I do not pretend to be completely unbiased or have no political leanings whatsoever having provided my personal details above and the background to this venture.

I hope that you enjoy reading the book and some of the contents resonate with you. My wish is that you agree, disagree, argue about and pull apart my observations but most importantly either individually or together with family, friends and work colleagues contemplate doing something about our world. Please take up the challenge and conceivably act for the well-being of all people today. I have no desire to put across a doomsday scenario or be too dramatic. I will have achieved a recent ambition in life should my meditations aid the constitution of a new model as to how we all live in the modern age and we truly witness **A Shift In Paradigm.**

<u>SYNOPSIS</u>

- We need to consider the possibility of and avoid what maybe the **bankruptcy of humanity.**

- A dire need exists for a new kind of **manifesto for life.**

- I believe that there has to be and we can achieve **A Shift In Paradigm.**

THE PREAMBLE

We are faced with rapid changes and developments encompassing many fields at an ever increasing pace whether in our personal lives, businesses, jobs, social contacts or friendships. External factors affecting us include:- the media, our nation's economy, political alignments, global climate change, terrorism and new forms of war – society hardly seems to be stable and comprehensible. Frequently we hear phrases such as:-

- They really must do something about it.
- What has the world come to?
- Why do people have to behave like this?
- Is there any good news around?
- People do not seem to have any values these days.
- Things move or happen too fast for me to understand.
- What can I do about it?
- Why can't people use some common sense?

We continually hear from politicians, businessmen and the media:-

- We will do everything we can.
- Your call is important to us.
- We put you, our customers first.
- You will remember of course.
- We have launched an enquiry – *a particular favourite of my wife and myself!*

MY ASPIRATIONS

With this book I am endeavouring to:-

1. Raise key issues for discussion.
2. Facilitate the starting up of dialogues and set in motion deliberations amongst families, friends and work colleagues.
3. Proffer my observations and, where I feel able to, outline solutions on these topics.

There is no intention to impart detailed technical knowledge or specialist coverage relating to any field, rather my assessment of these pivotal matters. There are numerous experts in each sphere who are well-qualified to and adept at putting forward in-depth information and so take up the reins, if they so choose, from here on in. I am motivated to put out there, my thoughts on a whole range of subjects that impact upon us and for everybody to address these worries. Individuals who are experts in their field can hopefully be enticed to expand upon these issues which I have dealt with only sketchily in most cases. Such professionals can refine the ideas and theories put forward into something more coherent – what follows is all being well, some of the raw material required and founded on what I perceive is behind the more superficial issues and policies which we all come up against.

Recently, on account of ill-health, I have retired early from work, but certainly not from life. These changed, unfortunate circumstances, have provided me with a rare commodity today – TIME. I have pondered on our lives at the start of the second decade of the 21st century – the positives and negatives according to what values and thoughts I believe the overwhelming majority of people subscribe to. Overlaying all of these principles, ethics and morals is a belief in and hankering after **realism, common sense and structure for our lives today.**

LET'S DO AN INTERNAL

During my reflections I noted and wish to stress that our society incorporates many positives worth mentioning in these first pages of the book. Many of us enjoy good lives as compared to what people endured just a couple of decades ago, let alone in previous centuries. Aside from some prominent examples provided below, we have witnessed enormous benefits accruing to many people in the fields of medicine, nutrition, wealth accumulation, modes of travel, spirituality, charitable work, the arts and entertainment, sports activities, space exploration together with scientific discoveries.

Referring to England, where I was born and have lived all of my life so far, we can be encouraged by much of what is experienced that is either specific or associated with our island nation. A particular example comes to mind as per a conversation I had with a client some years ago. He told me during a meeting that as a place to live in, England possesses many positive attributes that we do not always appreciate. He suggested that rarely do we come across extreme climatic conditions like hurricanes, earthquakes, volcanic eruptions and monsoons or riots, civil disturbances, rigged elections, police brutality and lightning strikes. My elder son who now lives abroad, frequently comments that what he misses about life in England are:- general politeness, orderly queuing, the Royal Family, pomp and ceremony, the City (as in London) and it's environ together with our well-known green pastures.

POSITIVES

- Medical breakthroughs for scores of life threatening diseases.
- Cheaper and easier air travel to and from many destinations around the world.
- The internet and communications revolution.
- Longer life expectancy.
- Increased understanding of the universe and building blocks of life
- Wide choice of consumer goods and services combined with a variety of retail shopping outlets.
- The ousting in recent times of many autocratic and dictatorial regimes across Asia, Africa and South America.

I appreciate that a substantial amount of the text in this book relates to problems and pessimistic aspects of how we live and the world around us. I am not attempting to put forward a balanced viewpoint or hold out answers in many cases. My profound disappointment is evident and intentional, since we have neither solved many drawbacks from the past or come to terms with the impact of new phenomenon.

NEGATIVES

- Debt at unsustainable levels, economic meltdown, and an increasingly complex financial world that we inhabit and for the most part, do not comprehend.
- Multiculturalism misinterpreted and part of society together with the resultant problems that are manifesting themselves throughout the world.
- Climatic change like the melting of the Polar Ice Caps, more extreme weather occurring in many parts of the world and general global warming.
- Rising obesity amongst young people in many so called "Western Countries".
- The perceived breakdown of law and order especially in countries with democratic governments.
- Excessive power of the media.
- Sexualisation of children and adolescents.
- Terrorism as a means to promulgate a cause.
- Religious intolerance, still widespread today.
- Corruption endemic amongst many people who we look up to and rely upon.
- The quest for instant recognition, fame, financial reward and a place in history driving many, but by no means all, youngsters to ever greater lengths for such purposes and often much disappointment. Serious ill-health and even suicides have been the outcome on occasions of such behaviour.
- Wealth increasingly concentrated in the hands of few people such as

billionaires, oligarchs and tycoons who can and usually do dominate decision making affecting millions of lives worldwide.

- Lack of and obsession with time for many people leading to mental health conditions so prevalent in our society today – depression, anxiety and stress blighting people's lives and even leading to death in some cases.
- Ever more cruel and baser forms of torture applied to people who are kidnapped, taken prisoners in the numerous wars taking place around the world or just due to their belonging to a particular faith, embracing a particular culture or their sexuality.

These are just some of the well known psychological and associated problems which we progressively encounter. *"Time wait s for no man"* has never been more apt than in this present age. Sadly in this context, communications are both instant and widespread whilst of course bad news travels faster than good news, combined with the availability of graphic illustrations relating to death, injuries, explosions, torture and war makes us all feel despondent and even defeatist.

We must learn the lessons of bygone days since as often quoted *"history repeats itself"*. Were people, and our leaders in particular, to analyse, and properly absorb past events we may not have to witness and endure the awful happenings and tragedies which are daily occurrences around the world. Collectively, mankind should pose the question "Are we really such a developed society, far advanced and so much better off than in previous epochs?"

I believe that listed above are the principal issues confronting us and which we routinely hear and read about. Many citizens have lost faith in politics and politicians, banks and bankers, religion and religious leaders and generally people in positions of authority. Habitually feeling let down, and distrustful of individuals who we normally look to for guidance, we predominantly incur feelings of disappointment and even desperation. No one person, particular period in history or social, economic, and political system has all of the answers or even faced head on a society's problems and this is no different today. Utopia can be sought but in my view never achieved and no individual in history, alive today, or who is born in the future will provide a panacea for all ills. We should expect in my opinion with our levels of education, health, technology and general choices in most fields to be "doing much better than we are".

Are there individuals in the world who can and would like to try and initiate changes which people can benefit from, I often ask myself? Young, middle aged and elderly, professional and lay, moneyed and those less well off, healthy and less able-bodied, I believe that we do have people on planet earth willing and prepared to come forward and act now. Many of the existing leaders have been discredited, viewed as tainted and failed to afford the solutions urgently required. Most of us generally feel disengaged from these people and their pontifications. Our world has reached a juncture at which persons who have the appropriate talents should make themselves known and be the architects of all our futures. I hope that what follows inspires people to steer us along an appropriate path for our happiness and survival.

Inevitably you will come across an overlap in certain areas, since my comments are germane to more than one part of the book. I make no apologies for this as it is appropriate to stress points under different and often related headings, since they are applicable within different contexts. The subject matter of the book is interlinked, aiming to deal with the foremost talking points of our current age and the substance based upon my awareness, knowledge and deliberations in each case. Some of the content will be viewed as controversial which is necessary since we cannot all agree and that is healthy and important for this book to succeed in it's objectives. Being diplomatic and *"sitting on the fence"* have in part led to many of our problems now before us.

With a book of this nature, the content becomes out-of–date almost immediately after if not actually before publication or at least overtaken by events rapidly. I expect that when reading about some of the items, there will have been developments occurring and other issues arising from what happens in our country and the world daily. The central themes will, however, be pertinent since many are in need of long-term deliberations.

I do not wish to be derogatory about any individual, political party, line of work or business, country, faith, culture or those who have lived in the past. I am seeking to engage readers in what I am convinced are the primary themes for humankind today. Possessing a differing outlook on life is what distinguishes us all, but from my observations, it may surprise you to learn of just how many issues and possible remedies we do all in fact *"see eye to eye on"*.

The analysis and solutions put forward pertain to England, although I am of the opinion that they will also apply to other territories and their populations. We are all part of the human race with similar needs and objectives. I hope that in going through the following pages you can determine where you stand on the most pressing issues of our age.

<u>SYNOPSIS</u>

- For the benefit of us all I am **seeking realism, common sense and a structure for our lives today.**

- Initially we must analyse and determine what is right and wrong with society today.

- The book's contents relate principally to England.

- Bear in mind the tendency where "*history repeats itself*".

- People from across the spectrum have little faith in and are suspicious of any utterances by current political, religious and business leaders.

- In order to be part of a movement for change and start dealing with the fundamental issues that need dealing with, are you prepared to come forward and act now?

<u>HOW TO ENGAGE WITH THIS BOOK</u>

There are opportunities for you as the reader to input your views on the topics covered throughout the book and maybe even participate in changing our world. I hope that you benefit from joining in with the assignments scattered amongst the following pages. Active engagement will hopefully enhance your reading experience and enable you to discuss the themes with other people in your life.

Symbols and their meaning are set out below:-

"Quotations and Sayings" - details contained under the REFERENCES Section

Exercises To Focus The Mind On

Questions To Ponder

Answers to the questions are to be found at the end of this book.

1. OUR MONIES – FINANCE IN THESE MODERN TIMES

WHAT IS GOING ON?

At the time of composing this book, we are truly into unchartered economic waters with politicians, business people, consumers, in fact everybody having to come to terms with the aftermath of a worldwide banking and financial crises. I sense that a whole new vocabulary has sprung up over the last three years or so to cover the events and try to explain how and why they have occurred. Established notions and practices have been dispensed with whilst new theories developed almost at will. Everyone is struggling to grasp a new national, european and world order regarding debt, interest rates, savings, mortgages, pensions, taxes, international trading, accumulating as well as conserving wealth, budgeting not to mention the financing of the private and public sectors.

We are becoming familiar with terms like the "need to balance our economy" and requiring a "painful readjustment" along with the often quoted saying "reducing the public deficit". Other popular phrases include going through "choppy waters", reference to people being "out of the labour market" and "going for growth". Perhaps one of the most telling amongst the new idioms is "Quantitative Easing (QE)" which is a monetary policy used by central banks to stimulate the national economy where they buy financial assets like government and corporate bonds to inject a pre-determined quantity of money into the economy. Effectively via QE the Bank of England (BoE) has created new money for use in the economy. We might know this more commonly as "printing money" although bankers and politicians vehemently deny that this is the meaning of QE.

People in many fields of work not just bankers, seem to have a need for being incentivised, are bonus orientated, possibly seeking tax avoidance (not evasion) and habitually pursuing "value for money". Permit me to **assign money to it's proper place – a medium of exchange.** We should not worship, overvalue, squander or lose it. **People lie, view and die for it**.

Greed in various guides seems to be a mantra via which many business people live by, a theme which features heavily in the 1987 drama film called *"Wall Street".* The Member of Parliament (MP) expenses scandal and levels of bonus and pension contributions paid to many company executives and senior directors, are just a couple of examples relating to this type of behaviour. The overwhelming number of employees and self-employed people have to make do with a static level of income in the present economic climate with the prospects of job losses and business failure to contend with. We have all heard of the quotation *"money is the route of all evil"* and whilst I do not subscribe wholly to this, it does underlie and influence much decision making and behaviour mostly to the detriment of us all.

Avarice and an insatiable appetite for all aspects of remuneration have permeated politics, sports, the various fields of entertainment and our public services. We appear to have lost sight of determining and being satisfied in other ways or as the current modus operandi is "measurement of happiness". We fail to identify with and quantify in any meaningful way what a job or activity is worth and constitutes a "reasonable reward". Consider the following:-

- Being top of the earnings pile.
- "Keeping up with the Joneses"
- "Ripping off the taxpayers"
- Falsely claiming off insurance policies (which is fraud and a criminal offence).
- Transferring to a different football club mainly if not entirely for higher wages.
- Targets applied in order to qualify for a financial benefit affecting people in the public sectors and not just private enterprise. I refer here to parking wardens, schools, train operators and ambulance drivers – generally with regard to times, numbers of people involved, costs per unit and various other criteria that is financially orientated.

The Olympic Games came to London in the summer of 2012 and were a huge success on all counts. I thoroughly enjoyed the TV Coverage and like many other people, were proud of how our nation staged this great event. I do feel, however that the Games also represented a giant financial spectacle with almost saturated media coverage before and during this extravaganza about costs, profits, sponsorships and ticket allocation regarding the monetary benefits for those involved. The awarding of major sports events to a particular country is also symptomatic of monetary considerations. Examples are the World Cup for football being awarded to Qatar in 2022 and previously in 2010 to South Africa, which were accompanied by allegations of financial irregularity made by various interested parties for both of these events. Such assertions have also been made in respect of Formula 1 racing, yachting competitions and other sports extravaganzas, although I would emphasise that I have not come across any evidence supporting these assertions.

I am aware of frailties inherent in the human race, and those relating to financial reward are neither new or perhaps of the worst kind. I do maintain, however, that some have infiltrated into previously sacrosanct areas of our lives impacting on issues like morality and social cohesion. Incentives, sweeteners, taking a bung and similar terms are used for situations which can border on or actually constitute bribery and we may be talking about the providers of public services and even the heads of some countries.

GROWTH FOR WHOSE SAKE!

Expansion of firms is commonly measured solely by increasing sales, profits, dividends, turnover and such like - an obsession with today's company owners and senior personnel. In a recession or downturn surely it can be sufficient to just maintain existing levels in such a demanding trading environment. Even 10% or lower than a previous period measured is not inherently bad – why are we schooled to believe it is? For what reason(s) do we have such a preoccupation with continuing increases year by year for such data which is clearly not always achievable.

Business owners should strive for the maintenance of the status quo during periods of high inflation, an economic downturn or a banking crises. This sounds heretical but established doctrines must be reviewed if any economy is to flourish in the present era. Just retaining the existing workforce represents an achievement and perhaps can be considered alongside improving and possessing expertise in a current line of business. Maybe those who run companies should concentrate on ensuring that shareholders understand how receiving any dividends, can be a good return on their investment.

I am not suggesting an absence of creativity, the development of new markets or modern means to transact business. We must accept and indeed encourage progress. I am convinced, however, that the panacea of economic growth is neither practical or desirable to produce increasing profits, full employment, consistently low costs for borrowing, rising levels of turnover and satisfaction in the boardrooms and thereby ultimate satisfaction for private company owners at all times.

Economic growth is now the chief policy pursued by all political parties and spouted by everyone who is interviewed for the news or a documentary programme on TV. There is a pressing need to examine what growth people are referring to and exactly how this will necessarily feed through to job creation and more wealth which all and sundry consider is vital for us to climb out of the current economic mess the world's economies find themselves in. Increasing sales, revenue and profit are a laudable aim for businesses and in many cases will mean an increase in required staff and so help reduce the very high levels of unemployment that we are experiencing.

Growth can also mean developing markets overseas where that country's job market will mostly benefit, diversifying into new areas of business resulting in trade being taken away from another firm sometimes in the same region of the country. Pursued to the exclusion of all other considerations, growth might have negative connotations where business leaders fail to take proper account of moral and ethical issues relating to their workforce and how a firm should conduct itself, in the wider world.

In order to reach the required growth targets, companies may recruit people to work on low wages with the benefits and profits accruing mainly or even exclusively to the higher echelons. Following on from this, there will be a concentration of earnings and wealth even more into the hands of fewer and fewer firms and people. There might be a long time lag between investing for and achieving the rewards associated with growth - measurement of any success could be in years or even decades in some cases. There will be no immediate impact on the economy and people's finances for a long time, which is not always explained by the business leaders and politicians who promote this strategy so forcefully.

Maybe growth implies a quicker depletion of a particular resource which the world is already short of and instead of seeking growth, we need to find new ways to produce items or provide services that make better use of resources and spread the benefits more evenly across the population of a country or the world generally. Growth must be clearly articulated for all involved and not just deemed as the **holy grail for economic salvation.**

YOU CAN BANK ON IT

 Yes, I sometimes hark back to days gone by when people wore bowler hats and secretaries pencil skirts in the City, whilst the telephone receptionist was the first and most important point of contact at any financial institution. You may also recall when luncheon vouchers were a well known and utilised "perk" and of course, all that most people did on a train was read, sleep or just sit and avoid making eye contact with any other passenger. "We must move on" you may be saying out aloud since they were not always golden days and surely we are so much better off now. I agree that excessive nostalgia is to some extent unhealthy and misleading for each generation has to grapple with changes that often seem difficult to comprehend and adapt to.

The crux of the matter is that we should not abandon all that went before and appreciate how and why people or organisations operated in the past and when this remains befitting in our current age. Banks are a classic case where this was not taken on board and an illustration of the costs and problems involved when we *"throw out the baby with the bathwater"*. Moving away from their core business of looking after deposits from savers (individual and corporate) and lending funds out to them has led to the long-standing reputation gained for security, stability and sensible money management having been cast aside and maybe lost forever now.

Needless to say, as for many other domains, banking has not just changed but operates in new markets with a different emphasis and what can be called a new *"mission statement"*. Like grocery shops, chemists, TV Programmes and sport (inundated and preoccupied with money) banking is not what it was. This industry has expanded into other fields and incorporates diverse activities across numerous territories in the world. These long-established and reliable institutions were up until the 2008 banking and financial crises the bedrock of the UK Economy and most countries in the world. I recognise that several banks suffered financial difficulties leading to this unprecedented crises but for our purposes, will focus on just one – Royal Bank of Scotland (RBS).

The collapse of RBS and the subsequent bailout by the UK Government, was estimated to have cost the taxpayer £45 billion resulting in their ownership at 83% of RBS. At the time of writing about this disgraceful episode in banking history, nobody at RBS has paid any, let alone, the ultimate price for this debacle. There have been no criminal convictions, senior employees sacked, or much evidence of any real remorse. Indeed the former Chief Executive Sir Fred Goodwin and his co-directors have not been subject to any form of punishment by the Financial Services Authority (FSA) as the regulator or even struck off as Directors! Sir Fred as part of the bailout arrangement had to agree to step down, a course of action made somewhat more palatable by walking away with a substantial pension pot.

In accordance with other themes covered in this book, I muse on what sort of example this sets for our young people starting off in the workplace not to mention parents raising children to do the right thing and behave according to a set of values which are inherently good. We now have an established principle that failure of a large enough private bank will ultimately be followed by a rescue funded from the contributions of hard pressed taxpayers! I am aware that at the start of February 2012, it was announced that Mr Goodwin's knighthood has been revoked but bear in mind that the award in the first place in 2004 was for services to banking.

You might be forgiven for believing that "lessons had been learned" after banking and the practices involved were subject to reviews and much soul searching by politicians, senior employees at the major banks, BoE and the FSA. In January 2012, RBS Insurance was fined £21.7 million by the FSA in respect of staff at Direct Line and Churchill – BOTH INSURERS OWNED BY RBS who were found guilty of altering some customer files with forged signatures in an attempt to pass a regulatory inspection.

Coutts which is the bank famous for handling the Queen's finances was fined £8.75 million on 26th March 2012 for "serious, systemic" money-laundering failures. The FSA told Coutts which is now owned by RBS that they were lax in checking whether funds paid in by high-level, foreign politicians came from legitimate sources. In November 2011, Coutts was fined £6.3 million for misselling savings products linked to the collapsed United States (US) insurer American International Group (AIG). The fine in March followed a visit by regulators to Coutts in October 2010 and the FSA found that the failings identified has persisted for nearly 3 years.

I recognise that many other insurers and financial organisations regulated by the FSA have had some form of sanction imposed in recent years for breaches of the relevant codes under which they operate. The spectre of RBS again, however, falling foul of rules so soon after what some people were saying at the time of almost single-handedly bringing the UK Financial System to it's knees is deeply worrying for all who work in the financial services industry and consumers alike.

I do not pretend to either fully understand everything that has happened in recent years within the financial services industry or possess a magic solution to make it all better. I do, however, assert that "**greed is not good for anyone, even for the perpetrator**" and making amends for what has gone wrong should start from the top. The BoE and FSA must understand and discipline those at the most senior levels in financial organisations where their decisions on strategy, together with the products and services offered, cause financial loss to customers and even more so to the UK's financial system. Retribution must be swift and appropriate if we are to eventually restore everyone's faith in financial services.

FINANCIAL SYSTEMS AND MANAGEMENT

Excessive globalisation in conjunction with different methods of international financial transactions incorporating complex credit arrangements, causes misery and financial problems for many people in certain parts of our world. This state of affairs obtains usually in the name of "growth". Government policies for interest rates, taxes, and other financial instruments are implemented with regard to "the markets" is the customary justification applied. Markets are not some inanimate medium but consist of people who often pursue their own, financial self- interests. Trading is an integral part of a developing world, but hugely sophisticated and global economics do not always work in people's best interests in the developed or less developed nations.

There is a definite need for more long-term thinking and actions to be carried out in many fields. Property and equity investment as well as capital projects in both the private and public sectors should be evaluated over the long-term which should be a period of at least 10-15 years as a minimum timescale. Far too many decisions of major import are made on a short-sighted basis, which is detrimental to the very people who are due to benefit. All participants in such investments must be urged to fully appreciate how returns are generated on such financing ventures like the Wembley Football Stadium, Eurotunnel, possible building of a third runway at Heathrow Airport, widening of toll roads and motorways together with the revamping of hospitals and schools in monetary terms. Private investors in funds incorporating equities, properties, fixed interest securities, and those combining all 3 sectors together with some cash instruments also have to be considered over at least the medium-term (7-10 years). Too often the time span is unrealistic and a cynic may deduce geared to General Election timetables and such like political considerations.

Frequently the privatisation of certain companies, public utilities and organisations is put forward as a solution to all of the woes of a particular financial sector or even the whole UK economy. There seems to be an inexorable drift towards this "privatisation mantra" – why? The profit motive together with remuneration arrangements incorporating all sorts of inducements should NOT apply to "OUR public services" since we can all have need of the utilities and amenities involved from time to time and fund via payment of our tax and NIC. Some instances to consider are:-

- Hospital Accident and Emergencies (A & E) Departments.
- Scheduled rail and coach services.
- Policing.
- Local Authority Services – libraries, street lighting, regular waste collections and many others.
- Resources like water and various forms of energy.
- Defence forces.
- Sites of heritage and nature beauty.
- Museums of National interest.

I put forward the idea now which worked in the UK some decades ago, for a "Mixed Economy" incorporating elements representing the optimum for the production, distribution and consumption of goods and services. All economic, social and political systems – communism, socialism and capitalism together with their variations and all of the others which existed at some time or another, have their merits and drawbacks. No single structure is perfect for all peoples, all societies and at all times, they are appropriate and work for different aspects and periods of a successful economy. We seek to pigeon hole people as to whether they are inclined to be left wing, right wing, in the centre, leaning slightly to one side or another (even when sober) in terms of their views and policies which they support.

We hear constantly today about the drive towards more "EFFICIENCY" which is frequently quoted as a government policy. More often than not this is just a euphemism for "SAVING MONEY" and "CUTTING SERVICES". Presently in the UK and many other countries around the world, cuts in public services are being imposed on an already financially hard-pressed public. These so called "austerity packages" are of course decided upon by those who invariably do have money and hold down very well-paid jobs. I suggest that in these times of dire straits for so many people, they adopt the dictum **money, responsibility, accountability & humility.** How much easier it is to blazon the trail of making do with reduced public services, lower state benefits and less income to keep up a standard of living when you are not one of those having to cope with the affects of such fundamental transformations in our financial system.

SERVING THE PUBLIC – EFFICIENT OR NOT!

The National Health Service (NHS) has had billions poured into it by governments in recent years whilst improvements which have been made vary depending upon postcodes, the area of medicine involved and decisions made by the Primary Care Trusts in applying the funds provided. Her Majesty's Revenue & Customs (HMRC) has had huge amounts spent on a new computer system and a major outcome has even been amongst the staff (let alone the taxpayers themselves) confusion and numerous errors made together with the under and overpayment of tax due as a result of "computer errors". HMRC have also suffered an actual lack of revenue that the government of the day should have received and needed.

I have lost count of how many times the ownership of various train lines have changed hands, sported different logos and pictures painted on the train carriages and at some stations. At the same time commuters continually incur delays to services, lack of sufficient rolling stock and signal failures meaning increasingly unreliable and inefficient services to the passengers. In these and many other cases, money has been spent but not always **in the right manner, reaching the right people at the right time and leading to the right results – The 4 R's**

Contemplate if you may, to what extent, if any, education, public transport, policing, local authority services, healthcare provision and many other functions of central and local government should be determined exclusively by what I believe to be this ill-defined but contemporary yardstick. Efficiency is being put into practice by people with executive functions, to all aspects of our lives today but do we really know what is meant by and how any success in efficiency will be established?

To my mind, our world has demonstrated incompetence and waste on a grand scale in many ways recently. Some examples I quote may chime with you.

- Lack of progress in developing significant and cost-effective alternative sources of energy following the Organisation for Economic Development (OPEC) crises of 1973 and the increasing price of oil almost ever since. Money and the price of oil have dominated our economic agenda for nearly four decades.
- Appreciating how people use the power of the internet and social networking sites for evil and criminal means. There has been an absence of any real political consensus and rules across the world to implement effective legislation against such practices.
- Allowing debt at corporate and national levels to reach such extensive magnitudes.
- The failure of huge banks and financial institutions across the globe resulting in financial chaos, huge amounts of money involved in propping up these organisations and large-scale redundancies.
- Not providing adequate education and contraception to many of the world's poorer countries (despite momentous efforts by some organisations and individuals) culminating in a population explosion with millions of babies suffering and dying needlessly.
- Failure to ensure the proper use of our natural resources and protecting the environment for us and our future generations.

These failings reflect on us all not just our so-called leaders. Immense moral and ethical issues follow on from such weaknesses, which in financial terms are incalculable and partly accountable for some of the monumental social problems many people encounter today.

We are also being propelled towards undertaking everything on the cheap. Just consider for a moment:-

- Community Support Officers rather facetiously known as "plastic policeman".
- Having volunteers like the Territorial Army (TA) to be recruited sometimes replacing full-time, professional soldiers and services personnel.
- Many schools having teachers who do not have the PGCE (Postgraduate Certificate in Education) to know how to educate children and acquire the required skills.

These people do a great job and the criticism is not intended for them, but policies and a system which encourages them to perform a role which necessitates proper and often long-term training and investment of resources and leaves them open to danger and sometimes ridicule by those people who they are serving. I also feel sorry for the professionals currently undertaking those jobs, and consider it wrong to bring in any person who does not have all of the required skills and expertise to carry out duties alongside them.

INVESTMENT OR COST – WHICH WAY TO LOOK AT IT!

I worked in the training field for many years during which time I attended various courses to acquire knowledge of new products, changes to taxation and NIC, and general developments within the financial services industry. From decades ago I recall the debate concerning whether sending people off to a training event should be considered:-

- A cost to the business in lost time and earnings, or
- An investment which will pay dividends by way of increased income and profitability to the firm and individual employees

Invariably, the stance was the former denoting that many opportunities for the development of the business and individual's ability were denied. At best the decision to proceed with any training was taken only grudgingly with a remit for an almost immediate payback in monetary terms.

Sadly, the same line of reasoning still prevails at the highest level of decision in some companies. In many professions there remains a reluctance to participate in or start undertaking some form of continuous professional development usually known as CPD except where it is compulsory. Also, in many lines of work, we need funding for, and properly designed qualifications to be obtained, as a sign of professionalism and competence – something which I am aware is happening in more fields today than just a few years ago. Areas of work which would benefit all concerned for me are:- information technology (IT), Estate Agency, Debt Counselling, advertising and promotions and no doubt many more which you can think of.

I venture to suggest that one particular field where this would be novel but hugely rewarding for us all is the job of BEING A POLITICIAN. The qualification for politics should not be limited to holding a degree in political science, law, economics or any other similar discipline, but require a mandatory period of "on the job training" working alongside others who are already licensed and so incorporate "work experience". This sort of work placement or as we used to call it in my day a "sandwich course" wherever possible must incorporate:-

- Experience at local and national levels.
- Participation in debates and interviews for TV, the press and all forms of media.
- Working with people in a cross section of jobs in order to attain some grasp of how those who they hope to eventually govern live on a day to day basis.

PREPOSTEROUS I can imagine some readers thinking and **IMPRACTICAL.** How many jobs can you name where, in principle and often in practise, somebody can do their effective apprenticeships solely within a closed world of theory or at best with only limited real life experiences. Many of our politicians who join a political party in their teens or 20's go from university to local government, possibly also working for one or more quangos, sit on company boards as non-executive directors and act as consultants to companies. They are invariably from moneyed backgrounds which does not imply an inability to do this job only that they may not be best placed to comprehend many of the difficulties and stresses of modern day living.

My assertion is that much of our expenditure (private and public sector) is deemed a cost rather than an investment. In line with my contention here and those elsewhere in this book, think about how our political leaders and others perceive the following:-

- More police patrolling our streets and easily accessible to prevent the occurrence of a crime and deter criminal actions happening in the first place.
- Having a general hospital incorporating A & E in every town and city of whatever size or specific population level since prevention is better than a cure.
- Every train station in the country which is a form of hub or interchange with at least one other line or is busy as measured by a particular level of regularity that trains stop there to have a lift/escalator/ travelator and maybe all three. Also, somewhere on at least one platform or in the station concourse a heated, covered waiting room and facility to purchase hot drinks and bottled water.
- Airlines to pump out higher levels of pure oxygen during flights which

will help reduce the risk and occurrence of viruses and infections to passengers breathing in stale air and recycled germs. This will save on misery and lost working time for many people each year, although I realise will incur a higher cost base for airlines.

- For all construction and building work – think of longevity not just short-term periods and profits. Using better and yes, initially more expensive materials at the outset will save potentially billions of pounds by not requiring frequent repairs and even replacement – motorways, train tracks, potholes etc.
- Simplified or at least a more common sense system for tax and NIC so that there is less motivation and scope for avoidance and consequent lost revenue. Further advantages would be:-

  a) Reduced need for complex financial services products to save on tax.
  b) Tax saving arrangements can and often are misunderstood by the public and poorly promoted to them – usually best understood and taken up by those with more wealth and access to top professional advice.
  c) Less need for employing an abundance of inspectors and others to monitor people and the schemes involved.

INVESTMENT (and so decision making) should be gauged by significant health, ethical, social and environmental alongside the financial benefits. Here is an example of changing our perceptions and looking long-term at improvements that will flow to the well-being of so many people.

SIZE MATTERS!

Immense, supranational, all powerful organisations now exercise significant control over our economies. A recurring quotation is made in billions or trillions as a unit of currency which is incomprehensible to most people and unlikely to be accurate to the last pound, euro or dollar!

In England it is true that we have a "Big Society" but not the one David Cameron (our current Prime Minister) and the Conservative Party support as a policy. We inhabit a nation comprising massive retail superstores, all-embracing hotel chains, huge aircraft and ocean going cruise ships, enormous sports stadia and some large people! Size seems to be a measure of our advancement and progress as a society.

Should we mourn the loss of British-owned companies which we and our predecessors grew up with? Chocolate makers, car producers, major national and international airports, banks and building societies, insurance companies, train operators and various other industrial giants that are foreign owned now come to mind. Enjoying village and country life with individual shops foremost in the high street and small commercial units nearby, customers purchasing home grown products and using resources in and around our island is not going backwards. Big is not always beautiful. Few products or services can now be said to be "Made in England" and I venture that this trend is neither inevitable or even desirable. Is it inherently wrong that we seek to protect jobs and livelihoods at home and preserve our own culture?

I believe that deep down the leaders of all countries should adopt a similar approach and many probably want to do so, but feel constrained by international trade agreements and membership of assorted bodies worldwide. We must distinguish between incurring accusations of being economically speaking protectionist, racist or xenophobic by maintaining such a stance where we are actually just patriotic and realistic. Protectionist tendencies are frowned upon officially, yet many countries do practice this form of economic activity to some extent and often via intricate financial arrangements.

Vast corporate empires and conglomerates function in many different countries and continents having undue influence over our lives today. There is a good case to be made for reversing this trend in many instances and the establishment or reintroduction of more local and accountable organisations. Focus should revert to the precept that "the customer matters" which is plausible, rather than terms like clients, stakeholders, patrons, purchasers – although all valid in the right context.

Probing the relatively modern concept of "consumerism", we commonly buy much more than is needed and whilst not all purchasers should be geared to necessities and treats are rightly part of what we look forward to and enjoy, there are downsides to note. Perhaps our buying habits ought to reflect more what we want and can afford at the time, since it would be a salutary exercise to consider our purchases compared with actual requirements (even with some self-indulgence included). The impact on personal and family debt of a change in emphasis as to how many of us shop may also be enlightening. There is no demand for an abundance of retail outlets located in almost every town or city and frequently more than one shop or store of the same name in larger locations.

I am not advocating that we diminish the variety in our lives and fully appreciate how the retail industry provides copious jobs and access to an extensive range of merchandise. Nevertheless, many shops are not profitable or ever likely to be. Developers and financiers are responsible for enormous retail parks which compete with small, well established local trading outlets and more often than not into the bargain the source of unwanted local traffic congestion.

At airports and other travel termini why have a preponderance of shops which encourage people to spend money and possibly incur debt – a major problem in society today. Furthermore, usually it is the designer shops taking up much of the floor space and generally selling merchandise towards the top end of the market. My experiences are that duty-free is not always the cheapest means to buy articles. Airports of course have a captive audience who themselves usually have time on their hands.

It must be the case that when travelling, people have already purchased and packed whatever they need although I do feel that retail outlets for emergencies like chemists as well as food and beverages are appropriate. Certainly, shop owners pay significant amounts of rent do help defray the vast costs these building projects involve and it is all based upon commercial considerations.

Perhaps, in preference there should be museums, art galleries, large play areas for children and such like, which can be accessed free or at a nominal cost. These alternative facilities referred to would occupy people for much longer than shops (I know that there will be exceptions where shopping takes longer and is more enjoyable) where a passenger incurs delays or just routinely arrive early to go through security and ensure that they are not late for the journey. The obsession which we have with consumerism means that almost all space in such buildings is taken up with shops.

YOUR VITAL STATISTICS PLEASE

I cannot fathom how people always seem to quote rounded numbers in billions or trillions of a currency in news bulletins, newspapers, TV interviews and various other media. I wonder what purpose this serves other than for the benefit of high powered business people, government ministers and a relative minority of mathematically minded individuals.   Can we really comprehend the magnitude of:-

- Sales this Xmas were £........billion.
- The Gross Domestic Product (GDP) of a country is now €.......
- Reserves of coal, oil or any other energy resource just found are valued at $...........billion.
- The additional government borrowing needed to service the public debt is £.........billion.
- The total debt of the Euro zone countries now stands at € trillion.

A great deal of forward planning is based upon these huge and surely inaccurate figures. With the pricing of petrol we always pay a rounded up figure when filling up. To quote an example, if on the forecourt the cost per litre is shown at £1.36.99 the actual price paid will be £1.37. I understand that petrol stations set their computers to round it all up thereby making a profit each time with consumers losing out.

At automated telling machines (ATM's) we are provided with higher notes of a larger denomination so for example where you request £30, the cash machine as it is normally referred to, will spew out 3 x 10 notes, or 1 x £20 notes and 1 £10 note. For £100 it will be 5 x £20 notes. You will not receive any £5 notes and as we all know once you break into a £20 or even £10 note and obtain change as coinage, somehow this disappears quickly. This of course is not the fault of ATM providers but it would help if we could have lower denomination notes amongst the monies dispensed.

There always seems to be more impact whenever we are told that so many thousands of people will be made redundant as against hundreds or scores of people. In a similar vein, we are usually told towards the end of the year about train fare rises becoming effective in January of the new year and how commuters face increases of 10% or 18%. Upon closer examination, the rises are different for each train company and across different routes, with some much lower than these headline figures.

We should always be mindful of the famous quote by Benjamin Disraeli *"lies, damned lies and statistics"*.

I. O.U (I owe you) – DEBT ON A GRAND SCALE

Specific mention must be made at this juncture of the debt which countries have run up and, in particular, those of the Euro zone and the manner by which they actually relate to people living in England. Without doubt, all of us are entitled to a full, independent enquiry into the current national debt, bank debts, our public sector deficit, and what the Euro zone owes and to whom. Those in authority must examine thoroughly and explain to everyone, why so many economies and organisations have incurred such high debt levels.

The general public are being asked to pay off such debts via increased taxes and NIC, cuts in public services, redundancies and job losses. Wages are reducing in real terms due to the effect of inflation, whilst modifications to pensions are ruinous for people's future income upon retirement.

Voters and United Kingdom (UK) residents as for other countries, have a right to know and understand by what means we have arrived at this appalling situation. A fundamental role of the nation state is to tell their citizens the truth. Who are the people responsible (within banks and other providers of finance, governments and quangos)? These organisations all comprise people some of whom should be held to account. The three fundamental questions are:-

1. How did this happen?
2. Who is ultimately responsible?
3. What is being done to prevent a recurrence in the future?
   Here is a case where we definitely need an enquiry to be set up immediately, report back promptly, deal in the simplest terms possible with the three questions above and be actioned not binned!

Debt is a deep-rooted issue which must be confronted, since it is no exaggeration to say that potentially our whole way of life is under threat! There are individuals out there who are answerable to everyone affected by this **disgraceful debt debacle** and must consider the impact on whole communities around the world.

Private individuals are being compelled to pay for what governments, large corporations, and financial institutions bring about and the resultant actions carried out over recent years. We learned that as at July 2011 the government of the United States of America (USA) had been struggling to have accepted by their political institutions an extension amounting to £14 trillion of credit and the Euro zone countries combined were in debt to the tune of over £100 billion! Voters have not authorised these measures and in most cases have never had such operations properly explained to them – yet they are bearing the brunt of the cost!

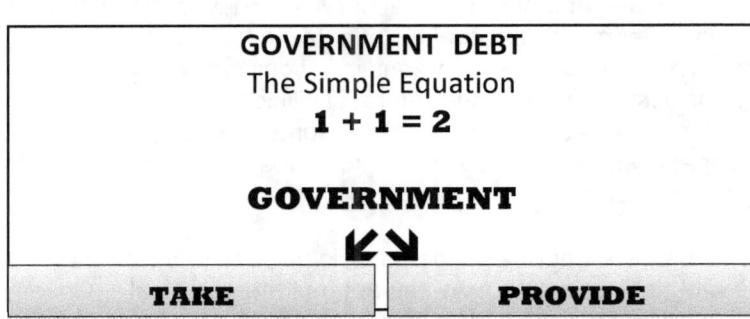

23

To fully appreciate how much these amounts are, can you write down numerically £1 billion and £1 trillion, and see how many 0's are involved.

All and sundry are experiencing the financial and social pain of debt in the world. Possible partial solutions to this money orientated blight on our lives are to:-

1) Make debt a subject taught in schools at an early age as part of financial matters generally.

2) Altering the buying habits of all concerned – governments, corporations and individuals to use credit in proportion to existing resources and clearly defined criteria to repay.

3) Adoption by the credit providers   (including and in particular relating to MORTGAGES) of the "capital and interest" method of repayment as against allowing just "interest only" deals. This will help facilitate moving away from "**the now society"** to a more balanced "**affordable society"**

4) Critically, evaluate the merits and drawbacks of advertisements and promotions which might adversely influence our behaviour and ability to become indebted.

Governments have permitted more liberalised advertising of gambling with a whole host of betting on TV Websites constantly on the small screen. We still see regularly on TV the marketing and encouragement for people to take out personal loans and more recently "pay day loans" with little or no formality and offering decisions within minutes.

Debt is a pivot of our lives today, and in my opinion, this situation is neither desirable or sustainable into the future. Drilling down a bit more into this parlous financial situation, I set out below some examples which we all need to consider and where I can, some distinct measures which can be enforced by the parties involved.

- **INDIVIDUALS** – credit cards, personal loans, overdrafts all at high interest rates and not backed up with any appropriate collateral. Governments need to pass legislation or issue clear guidelines for credit providers to follow which will forbid unrestrained borrowing.

- **HOMEOWNERS** – mortgage terms and conditions to be more strictly enforced where any payments are overdue to ward off financially risky borrowing and lending. This would lead, at least initially, to an increase in repossessions and attendant financial and social misery but I also advocate that specific account should be taken of lifestyle events like redundancies, divorce and serious ill-health. There should be a stipulated timescale before repossession applies and firm warnings during a "period of grace" to be followed by all lenders.

- **GLOBAL CORPORATIONS** – complex finance agreements across many boundaries, trading mainly if not purely on credit. Frequently, companies within a group are in debt to each other as well as external sources. The legal basis for any finance arrangements must be enforceable in one or more jurisdictions with severe punishments for individuals in power who seek to flout national and international laws.

- **GOVERNMENTS** – borrowing via the issue of various securities such as Gilt Edged Stock and Bonds since our political administrations are nearly always overdrawn. The financing of public services has become unstable relative to revenues (such as tax and NIC)) either received or even realistically expected.

- **COUNTRIES** – trade deficits regularly quoted in negative terms and figures.

DEBT STRIPPED BARE
LEADS TO

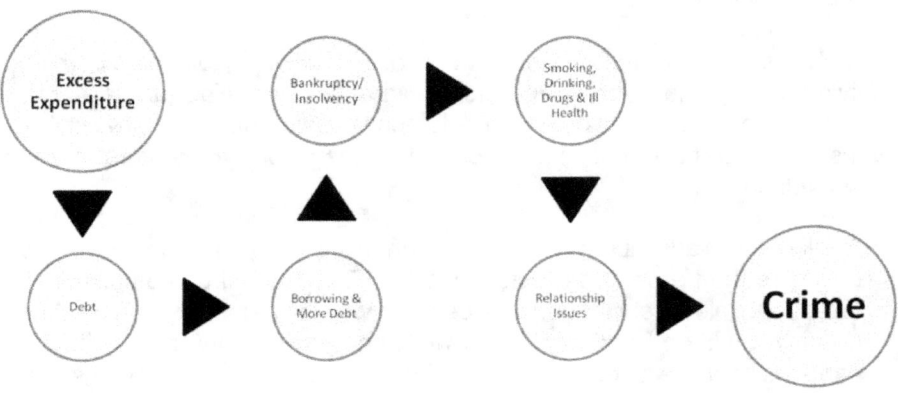

GIVE US A JOB

We must ensure that the current and future generations of young people are not lost in terms of having employment, providing income for themselves and dependants thereby being capable of maintaining a family. Our young people (generally defined as the 18 -25 age group) have in too many cases lacked a proper education, some are physically unfit and overweight, a small contingent indulge and have become addicted to bad habits within which a minority are involved in wrongdoing hence possessing criminal records. For these reasons and taking into account a variety of other circumstances, they may not be in a position to form stable relationships with a partner and are often disillusioned with society as a whole.

The solutions might be to:-

1) Restore university places to those pursuing an academic degree as best suited to this type of higher educational establishment.

2) Trade and professional qualifications to be attained at colleges as before which are geared up to and designed for obtaining diplomas and skills-based achievements.

3) Employers and businesses, wherever possible, looking to people born and living in England in preference to immigrants when filing job vacancies. This is not a case of being an Anglophile, xenophobic or protectionist just an efficient and sensible means to engage our youngsters into the workplace.

4) A minimum wage applying at a level enabling our young people to live on more than a basic subsistence level. This should be combined with realistic levels of social security benefits whereby teenagers and those in early adulthood are inspired to work and earn money rather, than as happens now in a lot of cases, falling into the "social security benefits trap".

5) Providing opportunities and most significantly financial incentives for employers:-

   • To take on jobs rather than penalising them via high rates of NIC.
   • Remove any requirement for contributions to an employee'

pension arrangement and savings for their retirement.
- Introduction of a simple, easily calculated government subsidy to hire them for a reasonable timescale – at least 12 months.

Targeting for motivation and reward is fundamental for job creation since it is clearly difficult for many to climb onto the "jobs and housing ladders", and also a better approach to the problem, offering dignity to this sceptical group of people that they can achieve something like everybody else. Too often we hear that they feel outside the mainstream of society since many young people face at the outset a life of poverty. Subsequently, in the springtime of their lives, this generation are confronted by and have to endure reliance upon their family, the State or loan finance – sometimes all three combined. One of the most incisive abbreviations of recent years has to be *NEET – not in employment, education or training* truly shameful.

There has to be a "sea change" in our thinking and how we operate in society. Employment, in addition to income, provides somebody with:-

- A purpose in their life.
- Important topic of conversation and something by which we currently define people.
- Scope to make a contribution to and feel part of the world around them.
- Help ensure that they are productively occupied to everybody's benefit, not least theirs.

Crucially, to avoid health-related, social and economic upheavals, our leaders should be compelled to address this issue as a top priority – we do not want to be responsible for the **"lost three" - lost employment, lost income and lost ambitions.**

JUST THE JOB

People must be urged to do and rewarded for performing a worthwhile form of employment as against what many other people (including myself) would call a "non-job" for example in many administrative and servicing situations in both the private and public sectors. There is no advantage to be gained by any party where a person is taken off the record for entitlement to Jobseekers Allowance (JSA) or Employment and Support Allowance (ESA) and placed in some role where they do not make any contribution to the firm as well as gaining little knowledge or experience of work. Taking on a job for people who have been out of work for a period of time must be viewed as beneficial to their community, family and themselves financially and otherwise as suggested above.

A variant of the old Marxist/Socialist Philosophy is the concept of all jobs having if not equal, then valuable benefits to society and so the reward should be commensurate with how significant this is to us all. I am not promoting that we pursue such a strategy in this country (or elsewhere), but mention the concept in the context of the unemployed taking on such all-important jobs as postmen, refuse collectors, lollipop persons, shop security personnel, street cleaners, local park attendants, typical so called "blue-collar jobs" which are vital for the proper functioning of our civilisation. It is paramount that potential contenders for these jobs receive the appropriate training cost-effectively to society as a whole and themselves, implying some form of pre-determined and easily understood financial arrangement. Deriving a livelihood from performing these and countless other forms of work is far better for all involved – primarily the individual themselves than relying on state benefits and however unwittingly, some reliance on an external source of finance.

Positive action implies a country's resources being utilised in a proper way and whilst not wishing to label anyone in this manner, the talent, enterprise and ability of each individual is the most valuable resource we have. Parks and open spaces, wastelands, libraries, clubs for disadvantaged people and many more such examples cry out for staff and they should be PAID STAFF. There is no merit in suggesting that your compatriots engage in some form of work out of pure altruism or as a punishment for being on state benefits for too long.

We all need money to function and far better to be received in return for performing something worthwhile. Governments must be instrumental in the availability of such jobs and not just continue to promote the merits of the private sector as if by some type of magic this will sweep up the millions of people currently out of work. We need to alter our perception of administrative and servicing jobs being in some way higher-grade and worthier than what today are still seen as menial and unskilled work.

May I stress that I refer to able-bodied people who are keen to work and the victims of the economic situation, cuts imposed by central or local government, company strategies and financial considerations in the private sector together with the lack of employment opportunities for a lot of people around the country. Individuals who cannot work due to ill-health and similar considerations should remain eligible for, and continue to receive for as long as necessary, state benefits and financial support from their communities.

I have no desire to delve too deeply into political philosophies as such, only to the extent that they impact on the purpose of this book. Consequently, many people currently work in complex and obscure jobs taking home very high earnings. We often struggle to understand exactly what contribution they make to our world and the value of what they do. Indeed, a common strand of thought is that some (but of course by no means a majority of) professional people (solicitors, accountants, financial advisers, bankers and investment management personnel) over complicate our world with the products and services which they develop and market to us.

We need people undertaking all forms of work in a modern society and the vast majority of professional and other people are needed and deserve the remuneration that they receive. I am mindful, however, as to how some individuals in those occupations mentioned here have played some part in the global financial crises which we are still reeling from.

Everyone needs to know that their neighbourhood is safe, clean and attractive to live in and our public services are properly staffed and to use a famous political term "*fit for purpose*".

We know that our current UK Government believes in "the big society" which I would strongly argue is just a means to procure:-

- Free labour to use an old, but well understood term.
- More involvement in charitable work which many people, where they can, already undertake and are offended by politicians who feel the need to categorise such work as a specific policy or encourage us to take part in such activities.
- Use a great sound bite which is nothing more than that.

There is clearly a massive focus on cost-cutting yet people are paid, not usually through any fault of theirs as is commonly maintained, to be at home, when they are perfectly able to perform services that are desperately needed. I surmise that retraining and performing a range of different jobs during one's lifetime is likely to be the norm from now on compared to the past where it was common to have a "job for life" or maybe change course infrequently. Learning new tasks and working in various environments will be an integral part of our lives and should be stressed to students at schools and colleges. We need to be prepared to accept this fundamental change to how we work and appreciate the benefits to our country as well as ourselves – an example of the desperately needed long-term thinking.

LET US ALL *K.I.S.S. (Keep it Simple, Stupid)*

A well-known phrase in sales and management. This is essential for people to understand and buy into programmes that deal with our economic woes – debt reduction, stability for the worldwide financial system, the Euro crisis, individual, state and company pension rights to name just a few. Also, due to the significant effect on all or our lives, grasping the personal, business finance and monetary statistics quoted such as measuring inflation, economic growth and the public sector deficit is essential and should be incorporated within the school curriculum as argued elsewhere in this book. Obviously, these are complex concepts justifying the use of specialist terminology on occasions but citizens must be able to follow the issues and proposed solutions.

Some instances where K.I.S.S is imperative are:-

- Adoption and use primarily of one measure for inflation that consumers can be familiar with. Some in current use are appropriate for different groups of people at various times.

- Social Security Benefits – claimants and everybody paying NIC should be able to comprehend the benefit amounts, eligibility, tax situation, and payment details.

- Means testing criteria – currently involving different levels, types of savings and income determining entitlement to a range of state benefits as well as Legal Aid.

- Pensions are now incomprehensible to all but a select few. Pension plans represent a significant part of many people's assets and their income in a later stage of their lives.

I fully recognise that there are limits to simplifying a lot of complex financial matters and it is impractical to dispense with all or even most of the phraseology involved. Many organisations have made great strides in the direction of making financial material (and that applicable to many other branches of knowledge) more comprehensible and there are some excellent websites now available to this end, including those which are government-sponsored.

<u>SYNOPSIS</u>

- The worship of money and what it can provide has become for many entrenched in their way of life so we should **assign money to its proper place – a medium of exchange. People lie, vie and die for it.**

- Do we really comprehend what growth is and why it is the policy most pursued by governments around the world. I wonder if economic growth should be viewed as the **holy grail for economic salvation.**

- Our banks and financial institutions have in large part brought about an unprecedented breakdown of financial systems and whose heads have often undertaken policies that are not in the interests of customers or the economy as a whole. We are reminded that **greed is not good for anyone, even the perpetrator.**

- Presently, an obsession with EFFICIENCY abounds – to you and I this usually implies cuts and saving money and so what we need is an approach that recognises the mantra **money, responsibility, accountability and humility.**

- Discussing how our public services are funded, we should bear in mind that any financial resources should be expended **in the right manner, reaching the right people at the right time and leading to the right results – The 4 R's.**

- All of us – governments, companies, businesses and individuals must reassess our approach to and seeming endless capacity for taking on debt. Understanding why the world is in debt represents the most important economic topic of our day and answers are urgently required regarding this **disgraceful debt debacle.** Collectively, shifting the emphasis from a **now society** towards an **affordable society** has to start immediately.

- Recognise the scourge of and deal urgently with unemployment amongst our young people – keep in mind the **lost three – lost employment, lost income and lost ambitions.**

2. HOW WE BEHAVE – SOCIETY AND OUR LIFESTYLES

WHAT A CARRY ON!

Some of the less virtuous   features of our conduct that I have mulled over are:-

- The recent MP expenses scandal.
- Absence of trust amongst a wide swathe of people in politicians and officials in the public sector.
- Misleading advertisements for certain products and services.
- Insufficient protection of children enabling them to "grow up naturally".
- Prevalence of the so-called "blame culture".

I am resolute that these and countless further illustrations of our activities are indicative of the standards which in my opinion, whilst erroneously in most cases, have become acceptable in this era. In the section below, I specify a handful of differing instances of our actions to illustrate the point being made. You will no doubt identify with some and possibly all of these and call to mind many more that you have come up against.

A sizeable proportion of people are inclined to be a tad more selfish now than in the past, solely to achieve what we believe is our entitlement as UK Citizens. We exhibit such tendencies in a variety of situations like:-

- Opting for the A & E Department of hospitals rather than wait often up to one or two weeks to see the GP (General Practitioner) since many surgeries are not open over a weekend.
- Pushing to board an overcrowded and possibly late-running bus or train
- Increasingly sending our children to private schools in order to provide them with a suitable education (often against as parent's our own political philosophy and inclination).
- In some cases people opting to pay privately for regular refuse collections and even in some regions, veering towards utilising vigilante squads.

There are positive choices as to how time is used (whether in or out of work) not all involving money. I am aware, as documented in previous pages, that for many people lack of jobs and income prevent participation in some activities. Repeatedly, however, we hear about boredom and that there is "nothing to do round here" from some youths. Local parks, libraries, the seaside (except costs of travelling to and from), natural sites of interest (many can be viewed without charge), museums (not all have an entrance fee) charity and helping people. There are low-cost travel options such as National Express Coaches together with cheaper fares on many train services. I appreciate that these activities might have conditions attached and some outlay is required, but with thought and maybe advance planning, there are pursuits can be enjoyed cost-effectively.

A phenomenon widely practised today is the use of abbreviations, which I cannot make sense of. When Susan Boyle became famous the media began referring to her as SUBO, Los Angeles which comprises only two words (and I am sure this applies to many other cities) is called LA. The financial services industry had a particular penchant for this tendency (and may still do) with particular regard to key dates, pensions, regulatory rules, investment techniques and descriptions of risk analysis. I fondly recall some measurements of money supply as M1, M2, M3 for example which were not to be confused with the motorways of the same name – I wonder which goes faster! Abbreviations are useful and time saving in the right circumstances but can represent laziness and their practice, in some lines of business and particular forms of media reporting, assumes prior knowledge of the subject.

In April 2011, temperatures were reported to have been 10 Celsius above average on some days which is fine, indeed lovely with regard to the climate for the long-suffering and sun-seeking inhabitants of our island. Headline grabbing weather data, along with many other realms, need to be understood in the right context since for averages to apply, figures must be higher and lower on occasions, in order to establish what is above or below average. Averages are quoted in terms of family budgets, countries' rates of growth in a particular category like the Euro zone, ages for contracting certain medical conditions, period of time equipment should last, number of hours sleep we ought to have each night – there are copious other examples that I could quote. People should not become transfixed by average figures but appreciate them for what they are.

One disincentive for me when going shopping at almost any outlet is the loud music blaring out – admittedly like many men it does not take much for me to dislike shopping! The music often starts as soon as you enter a shopping mall as my ears are assaulted with what is known as garage, house, heavy metal, hard rock, rap or electric pop music. People have different musical tastes and some might appreciate soul, country, reggae, classical, jazz or some other genre, but may I venture to suggest, in their own home and at their choice of time. I am aware as to how research demonstrates that the surroundings influence consumer's moods and so propensity to buy including music. My point is that any music should be in the background, at a level whereupon people can talk and be heard and certainly not containing swear words and offensive language generally, which I have heard on occasions.

Loud playing of music extends to many public areas where it is often difficult to find quiet parts to sit in or just contemplate your purchases or actions. A particular grievance which my wife has whilst commuting on a train is how loud some people have their MP3, I-Phone or I-Pod's playing and clearly somebody sitting next to them also has the dubious pleasure of listening to their music. When she looks at them as if to say "please turn it down" it is her who is deemed to be the aggressor, receiving a dirty look, or sometimes worse! I cannot help but wonder how much, if any, damage people who persistently listen to music at such close range, might be doing to their eardrums.

One answer to this persistent scourge of travellers on all modes of transport and applicable to many other bones of contention referred to in this book, is for the travel operators to launch a **respect campaign** similar to that we now have in football. Also, since many train services do have quiet carriages, more need to be introduced and not just fare dodgers, but those who fail to observe this requirement and play their music, must be apprehended and if appropriate, removed from the train at the next station. May be extend the concept of quiet areas to airports together with train and coach stations where these zones are clearly marked and signs stipulate that the rules must be adhered to.

A brief survey of different legal ages applicable to undertaking various functions in the UK demonstrates just how bewildering these are. A look at those recited below further enhance the argument for applying *K.I.S.S.* (mentioned in the previous section).

See how many of these you can state correctly.

1. Purchase alcohol in a pub, off-licence, shop or elsewhere
2. Voting in elections
3. Marrying with parent's consent
4. Marrying without parent's consent
5. Having sex
6. Becoming an adult in the eyes of the law and so criminally responsible for own actions and can be prosecuted
7. School leaving age
8. Pay tax and NIC
9. Leave home without parent's consent
10. Own an air rifle or pistol
11. Having a driving licence for most types of car
12. Give your child an alcoholic drink in the home
13. Be found guilty of rape and other sex offences
14. Be sent to a Young Offenders Institution or prison

These are the official British Board of Film Classifications (BBFC) for the UK:-

- U   **Suitable for all**
- PG   **Parental guidance**
- 12   **Suitable for 12 years and over**
- 12A   **Suitable for 12 years and over and contains moderate violence**
- 15   **Suitable only for 15 years and over**
- 18   **Suitable only for 18 years and over**

- R18   To be shown in specially licensed cinemas or supplied only in licensed sex shops, and to adults of not less than 18 year

I have seen many films which I consider totally inappropriate for these categories meaning that that they contain swear words, partial or full nudity or some sexual references and levels of violence shown that justify a higher age rating. I am not seeking to be priggish and recognise the rights and merits of youngsters enjoying and recognising a wide variety of experiences via the cinema, DVD's, videos and other such like transmissions. All age groups deserve exposure to real life often brilliantly portrayed in the movies, and also some TV offerings. Also, I acknowledge that all children (and some adults) mature at different ages but in too many instances, there is just gratuitous sex and violence involved.

Consider whether there are any current adverts that you deem to be unsuitable for the media involved, time aired and intended audience.

Whilst recognising that similar restrictions apply to countries around the world, it is the difference in ages and situations which are often illogical. The above is a summary – there are many more minimum legal ages applicable to certain activities and even sub-divisions involved under each age. Some farcical scenarios come to mind for example a young person can work, pay tax and NIC at 16 but not vote in a General Election before age 18, may have sex at 16, not leave home without a parent's consent until 17 and not marry without their consent until age 18!

FIDUCIARY, YES I AM REFERRING TO YOU!

We live an age where progressively people cease to believe and trust in government ministers, local authority spokespeople, employers, company officers and even religious leaders. This state of affairs prevails since a proportion of the aforementioned people either are, or at least come across, as insincere failing to follow the principles which they claim adherence to personally. I contend that misuse of public funds, failing to provide full information to the general populace as well as hiding behind a range of excuses for one's individual deeds are grave issues indeed. Such misdemeanours should be subject to more severe punishment than is the case now.

People in positions of power who often exert considerable influence over our lives need to answer the questions raised by interviewees – straightforwardly. Listeners and viewers ought to have faith in what they hear and see. Most court proceedings should be accessible to the masses being televised or available via the internet, especially where there is clearly a wider public interest involved. We must have confidence in the legal system, the judgements made and punishments meted out to offenders together with instances when cases collapse and how people conduct themselves when under investigation.

A democracy requires **T & C (trust and confidence)** by all of the country's inhabitants in the people who wield any form of authority over them and enact the laws of the land. Unfortunately, some persons in such positions have lacked conviction and been defective in their guardianship of our country's affairs. This situation leads to profound implications for the social fabric of our society, ethical behaviour of many people and not least, the impending rise of extreme political organisations on the far left and right. In particular, we are witnessing such movements making headway at the expense of a democratic government and in some cases actually destabilising the core aims and functions of an elected and constitutional government. We all have to be mindful of such developments and conduct ourselves in a law-abiding and righteous manner.

Corporate strategies increasingly involve the restructuring and financial reorganisations that are often a euphemism for redundancies, wage reductions and attempts to avoid tax by relocating premises and trade overseas. There is a clear case to be made for plain speaking and ensuring that the intended audience are able to understand what is being said. I frequently mutter to myself (it's alright I am of sound mind at least for now) what a load of baloney, or something to that effect! My eldest son, who has been known to scoff at my language, says to me "and for those of us who speak English". Our leaders have a duty to communicate wherever possible in a **clear and specific manner** and not hide behind jargon and concocted statements, whilst also accepting responsibility for their actions in the event that these impact unfavourably on us.

IS THAT YOUR MAKE-UP?

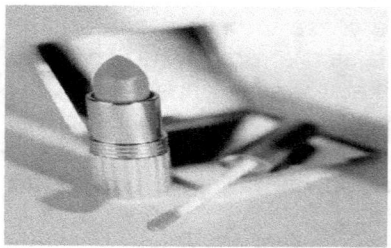

More than superficial cosmetic treatments – we need to have integrity and ethics as part of our persona. *"The buck stops here"* should apply whereas it appears all too often an avoidable concept for many of our leaders and a host of other people. Beauty products provide a veneer of prettiness and allure, and have been used by women (also men in some cultures) going back thousands of years and continue to be a force for good and basic to many people's everyday lives. The analogy here is the extent to which some people should look at a mirror and probe their underlying personality, temperament and disposition and determine who they really are.

The religious and social concepts of personal responsibility and accepting the consequences of our own actions and decisions must be embedded in us at an early age constituting a fundamental part of children's education. An increasing tendency to blame others for what happens is now widespread, and even more prevalent is the custom of having endless investigations, employment of special consultants and advisers and of course – enquiries!

We are all capable of doing wrong and this fallibility must be recognised. Being true to ourselves, family and colleagues is a virtue which has been sadly lost or at best forgotten by plenty of people. A vast amount of time and money could be saved if people more readily accepted their faults, benefiting all of us in the long-term, so that we can live by well established maxims. Good and evil exist in all human's make-up but for some mortals actions taken transpire as vicious, hurtful and corrupt. There must be recognition that proper education, being raised in childhood in a conducive environment together with knowing who we are **under the body's bonnet** will help towards people having the right balance and appreciation of their self.

Many a time I have wondered about how some people conduct themselves completely differently in a work-related environment as compared to hopefully when at home with their family – or just not at work. This assertion emanates from what such individuals tell us and also those close to them say. I also hint at this issue in the chapter about family and educating our children in terms of how they are brought up. Reference here is primarily, although by no means exclusively, to our so-called BOSSES. To what purpose do normally nice people who we assume or know for sure behave admirably in any other situation, but when transposed to their place of work, become highly unpleasant when dealing with people who they consider to be their underlings. Do such individuals really do justice to themselves and how they were raised in their formative years?

I do not agree that such actions and ways of communications can always be justifiable as how you need to be in business or as frequently quoted, if you are not prepared to be ruthless then reaching the top of the greasy pole is out of reach. There are other and better ways to demonstrate one's credibility in a business environment. Do we bring up our children to be good people, morally and ethically, and as parents hopefully set the right examples ourselves, and then whoever you might be, as a boss operate in business, work-related relationships and our general dealings with colleagues, in a contrasting manner?

How come we are genuinely pleased to learn of people at the top in any business organisation who have risen to their position after starting work for them or a competitor at the so-called bottom, or where they always visit outlets throughout the business to speak with people at all levels, or are qualified and have worked in that particular field as against being a lawyer, accountant or business manager by trade. We marvel at how they are plain speaking, maybe use public transport and seem to have no airs and graces. Such a scenario is indeed to be marvelled at whereas, I would contend, ought to be more widespread amongst our top business and company personnel.

It behoves us to accept that having children is one of the greatest joys anyone can experience – male and female. "*It takes two to tango*" should be considered when we seek to condemn either or both parties involved when a child is born out of wedlock, to a single parent and where he or she is not wanted, aligned to everybody bearing personal responsibility for their actions. Let us be sure that we appreciate and understand some of the actions that each of us have been responsible during our lives and profoundly how a child is brought into the world in less than enviable circumstances.

Make-up enhances appearances and helps someone to have more confidence when facing the outside world but as routinely stated, is only skin-deep. Deeper down what makes us tick governs how we actually go about our lives and I fear that for a large number of people, it is not possible to just enhance the surfaces, and the requirement is to focus inwards and discern the thoughts, character and values by which their life is led. Understand ourselves first and foremost and then seek to make sense of others.

HAVE WE LOST OUR DIGNITY?

TV programmes like Big Brother, I'm a Celebrity Get Me Out of Here and other forms of Reality TV, now feature heavily in our programme schedules. Do these offerings constitute alternative forms of entertainment or just cheap programme making? These broadcasts could be deemed voyeuristic, serving no useful purpose other than to publicise people who are willing to embarrass themselves for some TV exposure and so called fame. Maybe you consider that the programme makers are just responding to their viewers requirements and tastes.

Reality TV, which can provide instant fame represents in my judgement a passing, but highly influential fad capable of eroding what real artists, who in the main learn how to hone their crafts over many years, achieve. I wonder how many of those who appear on reality TV will be remembered in a few years' time, let alone in decades to come. Surely they generate excessive hype whilst almost hero worship status is conferred on participants. For me it is debatable as to whether there is merit in continuing with music and drama schools during this time. In today's world you can be fast-tracked to becoming famous if not overnight, then within a few programme episodes at the outset.

An aspect of these programmes which is particularly galling as compared to many other, and in my opinion, quality offerings by TV Channels, relates to their funding. Reality TV is cheap since often what are referred to rather derogatorily as "C" class or even down to "Z" class celebrities are the contestants or involved in some way who receive no fee or only a small payment for their services since money is derived from high rate premium telephone numbers dialled in by viewers to make their choices. This set up may not lead to quality people necessarily being selected and eventually becoming winners and so affects all in the entertainment industry and contributes to the widespread view amongst people that TV has been dumbed down in recent years.

A form of reality TV which initially gained enormous popularity not just in this country but many others also (that has to some extent waned in recent years), feature contestants who are prepared to prostitute themselves in pursuit of fame by undertaking tasks which if not in poor taste and crude, then surely represent inappropriate behaviour. I refer here to "I'm a Celebrity Get Me Out of Here, "Big Brother" and Celebrity Big Brother

The 21st Century may be defined as the modern era, but should many of our personal activities be open to and monitored by all sorts of organisations allowing for justifications like security, health and safety combined with policing issues being duly addressed. We must be able and prepared to keep much of our individual lives confidential which should be axiomatic for: entertainers, sports people, and those who are generally in the "public eye". These people should not be cannon fodder for the media which appears to have declared open season on anybody who is remotely famous. Every day we witness the incessant media focus on individuals who are judged as "fair game" in what is fast becoming a **toxic strand of journalism.** My fervent hope for the future is that we pull back and let each person have their privacy intact.

This state of play in our world today also encompasses Google Earth, Close Circuit Television Cameras (CCTV), Speed Cameras and many more intrusions into our lives which are taken for granted whilst impacting on our privacy and how we go about our daily activities. Much of this paraphernalia could be deemed incompatible with some basic precepts of how we exist. Crucially, in England I have heard it said in news bulletins that we are "the most watched country in the world". In this case I wonder, has there been a demonstrable reduction in crime and general misdemeanours, a general feeling of well-being and safety in public places plus an economic and ethical return on the huge financial cost involved with what has been implemented across our nation?

In contemporary society there seems to be a leaning towards informality such as calling members of a family by their first name rather than mum or dad as well as aunty and uncle. This trend also relates to other groups of people like children addressing teachers, employees addressing their bosses whilst in some instances even doctors in communications with their patients. In my immediate family, the convention is followed by all concerned towards my wife and myself being addressed as mum and dad together with aunty and uncle. I have two sons and I have told them on various occasions, something that they have always treasured **"you are the only people in the whole wide world who can legitimately call me dad".**

Formality and tradition should be part of our world – we cannot always act in a non-conformist manner. Abandoning our established conventions tends amongst some people to usher in disrespect, no recognition for our peers and lack of some boundaries. How our youngsters specifically, but by no means exclusively, speak to people is a rudimentary marker of how we behave. Currently, we are in danger of "*throwing out the baby with the bathwater*" by which I mean old values and parameters which many of us grew up with and abided by.

There has been some debate recently on whether mums should breastfeed in public and whilst this right is now enshrined in Equality Law, is it appropriate anywhere or only in specifically designated places? I would argue (yes strange as a normal full-bloodied male), that surely this is what breasts were designed for and embodies their purpose in life, rather than merely representing objects of sexual desire predominantly for the male sex. No man or woman should be offended or embarrassed by this most natural act, after all nobody is forced to stare in that direction.

We witness in public more than adequate forms of sensual behaviour by some members of both sexes that is not actually called for such as cleavage-showing tops, almost non-existent skirts worn by women, tight and in some cases boar-constricting jeans, trousers and shorts worn by men and women. Also relevant here are men wearing almost fully open shirts or even parading around bare-chested and some lads walking around with their trousers half way around their buttocks! Men and women kiss and touch each other (gracefully in most cases) have been known to shall we say "adjust their clothing and themselves" in various ways causing amusement to some and undoubted embarrassment to others – normally their partners!

Once again, may I stress that I do not consider such clothing to be in any way improper, quite the opposite in fact, why should anyone hide who or what they are, deny their skin access to the sun (when it decides to come out!) or conceal their physique? Flirting and even some flaunting have been part of humankind since time immemorial and rightly so. It is, therefore, incongruous to view breastfeeding as anything other than commonplace.

Women who breastfeed are practicing an innate part of raising their baby not to say something which only they can, and many medical authorities encourage them to do. We see breasts in situations which are not always befitting so should be fully accepting of their application for the right reason. The mother alone must decide whether she wishes to cover up in any way and do whatever is best for her baby, herself and let nature take it's course.

DO WE BAT AN EYELID ANY MORE?

The past shows how humanity for the most part tends to vary from one extreme to another regarding events happening, the changing structures of society and what is and is not acceptable to us. I often reflect on how, in the last century we witnessed.

- The former USSR (Union of Soviet Socialist Republics) which was dissolved on 26 December 1991 and 15 new countries were formed, moving immediately from communism to capitalism.

- Football where maybe 20 years or so ago, the physical coming together of players would not even be deemed worthy of the referee's or their assistants' attention. Now such clashes warrant a yellow or red card and even police action in some cases.
- Going on holiday meant being away and taking a complete rest from work. On any beach, in a café, in hotel lobbies and at airports, people regularly use their laptops, tablets, iphones, mobiles etc to "be in touch" and continue working. Even whilst in transit, people often resort to these devices demonstrating that they are always available and in most cases, still working.

- In previous eras, we would dress conforming with our intended destination and address people according to who we are with. In these times we have dress down days at work, jeans are commonly the defining article of clothing for all situations, and ties if worn at all, loose around the shirt collar. Frequently, in a business or occupational environment there is a custom to call people by their first name – senior managers or company directors and professional people.

- Sex, violence, swearing and offensive behaviour to many people is rife on TV, whilst also being reflected in computer games, newspapers and "on the street" thereby being extensively in the public domain. In a bygone era this would have been unacceptable and hardly widespread amongst our younger people, except in private. The media is continually hungry for stories and articles on these subjects and many TV programmes contain such material well before the "watershed". Advertisements are especially prone to include partial or almost full nudity even if as is normally the case, where it is tastefully done and no private parts are actually on show. As the saying goes "SEX SELLS".

These are not necessarily all bad, but more accurately indicative of how swings occur from one end of the spectrum to another. There needs to be a "middle ground" which is rarely championed by people and any comments or criticism often draws an interpretation as being *a sign of the times"*.

YOUR MONEY FIRST

I find it both astonishing and frustrating how money orientated aspects of our lives have generally become. Let me enlighten you with some examples which you have probably come across and I am sure expressed similar sentiments about:-

- Parking at a railway station, which should be free encouraging us to use public transport, necessitates a daily charge which in my area is in the order of £4 – 6.
- Visiting a hospital to see someone or more worryingly taking your loved one there in a potential emergency, needing cash to get into or exit the car park.
- Some shopping centres like to make a charge to park before entering the mall and part with your money in the shops themselves. As a concession, you can sometimes park for a specified amount of time free-of-charge.
- Pay and Display machines for parking on many roads is now cashless and you have to pay via a mobile phone. This is hardly user-friendly for the elderly or people without a suitable mobile and when parking in wet and cold weather having to undertake such a task.

A further substantiation of this point concerns pay and display parking spaces or meters together with the looming wardens. I submit that by and large pure money raising is the raison d êtra for their activities. Where traffic control encompassing the freer or speedier movement of vehicles is required, then no cars should be parked there at all at any price as they cause congestion. Surely, it is a spurious argument to put in place such apparatus since in no way is this a traffic control measure but a tax for leaving your vehicle in a particular stretch of road. As an aside, wherever it maybe, I am lost as to why parking a vehicle should warrant being charged any money at all!

INSTANT PLEASE

We seem to live in a constant **now society** rapidly moving onto the next fad. For a significant number of people, their lives tend to be "consumption led" and for many individuals, highly materialistic as we move ever further away from how our parents and grandparents managed their affairs. Fame, tanning and beauty, fitness, making fortunes, food (pre-cooked, ready-made and fast) and many more instances spring to mind.

Widespread short-termism regularly encountered today, is epitomised by the excessive pressure to perform and this in turn leads to stress and related modern illnesses such as cardiac disease, strokes and cancers. Football managers being sacked quickly, public sector projects abandoned due to lack of funds or political will, football players representing their country due to club performances for one season or even less, are now commonplace occurrences. I also cite the instances of government ministers being appointed to their positions after only serving a short-term period in actual office and usually with no background or expertise in the field involved.

In recent years, there has been a tendency to make films and shows about people who are not only alive but usually still quite young. The shows about Blondie, Madness, Rod Stewart together with films relating to Mark Zuckerberg (the creator of Facebook) and Lady Margaret Thatcher are illustrations of this trend. There were at one time suggestions of a proposed film about the Chilean miners who survived their ordeal and Sir Elton John. What is the purpose, I ask myself, when there are so many other themes to explore and people who are sadly no longer with us.

I maintain that too much emphasis is placed on and credence attached to looks, fashion and the superficial aspects of products and services available which are mainly designed to create an immediate effect. Youth is the face of life in this day and age. Excessive focus on a celebrity culture and status which some people aspire to can bring disastrous results – cosmetic surgery, waif like models, anorexia and disappointment with failure on reality TV shows.

On contests, awards and other big TV Shows, the female host more often than not change their outfit at least once, if not several times during the evening. This is a sign of opulence which is unnecessary, especially in times of financial hardship for so many people. I do not suggest that the individual presenters are guilty themselves for this short-term use of a costume or that they should look drab, but keeping the same attire on for an event or evening is more fitting (no pun intended). Frequent wardrobe changes are another manifestation of immediately looking different.

I agree with the well-established means to improve a person's looks such as make-up, keeping fit and propitious angles at which a camera pans somebody. Most people want to be seen in the best possible light and feeling good about themselves is normal and desirable. I abhor, however, some of the more recent developments such as air-brushing photos which raises moral issues as to whether this borders on a type of fraud – trying to be seen as somebody who actually looks different to who they really are.

Witness the extravaganza which is the USA Presidential Elections where, irrespective of any other considerations, it is possible to attain the highest political office in the land and arguably most powerful in the world, via wealth, staged appearances, presentation of the individual self together with countless vague phrases which, in truth, could be uttered by almost anyone. I felt that Tony Blair when he was Prime Minister in this country famously tried emulating to some degree appearing very presidential and his wife Cherie arguably sought to be the First Lady of our politics.

Ageism is endemic in the media embracing actors together with TV presenters and those who read the news bulletins or weather forecasts. Should society tolerate such an obsession with outward appearances, consigning to the shelf those people who are judged as past their *"sell-by date"*? The situation persisting today entails the waste of our most precious resource – HUMAN BEINGS. Becoming older is natural and symbolises a positive facet of our world. We are living longer with life expectancy increasing so let us hope that the 1976 Science Fiction Film "Logans Run" does not become reality. Soon middle age will be 50 to 60 years old! Brad Friedel, Ryan Giggs, Richard Attenborough, Helen Mirren, Julie Walters, Meryl Streep, Clint Eastwood, Bruce Forsyth, Tony Bennett, Tom Jones, Tina Turner – take all that! Far from revering what is instantaneous let us acknowledge the continuing contribution these experienced people provide to our lives.

Can the earth afford our existence in line with the present level of resources and an estimate of those likely to be available in time to come? Are we acting morally as well as economically with this mode of behaviour – consuming at such a rate and so rapidly? Should we be leaving debts, diminished resources, potential famine and poverty on an even wider scale to the **family of the future world**?

Any attempts made by our leaders to take a longer-term view with regard to targets for climate change, the rate of deforestation, pensions strategy, countries participating in or starting up wars in various parts of the world and exit strategies are met with prevarication or downright failure to agree on any course of action. Many people's place in history would be more assured if their thoughts and actions at this moment in time are far sighted and do not just deal with the *"here and now"*.

ENOUGH IS ENOUGH - OR IS IT?

In many respects we are fortunate to be living more enriched lives than our predecessors. There is no need to feel bad about enjoying better sanitation, more wholesome food, healthier living conditions and easy access to many destinations around the world. We also live in an age where we can delight in our grandchildren not to mention great-grandchildren.

Deliberating on our living habits today, perhaps there are too many alternatives and selections to make in areas such as: food and drink, clothing, cars, electrical equipment, in fact for all sorts of products and services. Thinking about this, are we best served with so many TV channels often repeating programmes which have been shown recently on their own or a competitor's channel? I would claim that excessive choice might actually lead to confusion and lack of real satisfaction as a person can never know whether their selection is appropriate and beneficial compared to what else is available. In my experience in the realm of providing financial advice to clients, which I was at least up until a few years ago qualified to comment on, the choice of investment funds for savings, pension and life assurance-based plans for a lot of clients, mitigated against really meeting their requirements. The internet has of course facilitated an unprecedented array of choices being available at our fingertips.

People on TV can wear the same clothes more often, indeed many of us when going to work, official ceremonies, wedding and other celebrations do not have a new outfit for each occasion (although I understand many women would like to!). Do we really need so much attire as exists in wardrobes and bedrooms across the land? Consider how often we just throw clothes, shoes and so on away having become bored with them or they are deemed to be "out of fashion". Conceivably one positive outcome of this activity has been the rise and popularity of charity shops.

Possibly the phrase and apparent cure for lack of shopping known as "*retail therapy*" is a symptom of a deeper malaise affecting our society. We have developed a shopping culture with reports of the "must have this season" for items of clothing and shoes. New developments involving offices and or residential accommodation almost always include some retail outlets. It is simple to see why the high street is suffering reduced levels of trading – just refer back to that famous quote by Napoleon that we are "*a nation of shopkeepers*".

In the 21st Century, should people who are in jobs work so hard physically and mentally over such long hours sometimes spanning a six or seven day week? It must be the case that a maximum five day week is ample, especially as I cover in the economics part of the book, with such high rates of youth and general unemployment prevailing. Indubitably, working for 70% of the week is apt for us to restore the "*work-life balance*".

I have alluded to the topic of how small can be appropriate and "big business" is not always relevant with regard to economics. In accordance with putting a stop towards the seemingly inevitable casting aside of what is sacred to many folk in England, we must endeavour to recapture the lost features of our culture like:-

- The village and country way of life under such attack in recent years.
- Reinstate where already lost and generally bring back more lollipop persons
- Inaugurate trams back in more of our major towns and cities
- Ensure that entry to our museums are either free to all or possible with only a modest fee payable.

This should not be viewed as an outbreak of irrational nostalgia on my part, rather an affirmation of symbols and experiences that define our nation, bring in tourism and will facilitate an improved lifestyle for numerous people across the country. I feel that too much of England has disappeared in recent times, and not always for the better.

We are not European (except geographically), Western (except as a point on the compass) a first or second world country let alone third world, whatever these terms actually mean. All of us - leaders, citizens and business people should cease trying to pretend that we fit into any such classification or that it is in our national interest to do so. Moreover, let us be proud of our traditions and values whilst accepting that we do live in a world where we have contact with and are influenced by other environments. We identify many other nationalities by what they represent, how they dress, their cuisine, traits, pursuits, work ethic, laws and general demeanour. **Diversity exists all around us – there is no need to prescribe it.**

On a broader basis nationally, we need to financially encourage and support creativity and initiatives in the realms of science and art as against funds continually being cut back. Enough of our talented people in these fields have to date moved away from England and now seek new pastures abroad as they cannot obtain work here, or fail to earn a living commensurate with their qualifications and expertise. We must retain these individuals and in line with other themes, obtain a return on their education and not be short-sighted since it is relatively easy to reduce budgeting in this sphere. Long-term investment into projects can and frequently does pay enormous dividends to the country long-term as a whole which is a contributory reason as to why England is no longer a world leader in many technological research-based industries. It is imperative that we reverse this trend.

<u>SYNOPSIS</u>

- Consider how we conduct ourselves in public and launch a nationwide, all encompassing **respect campaign.**

- There is a distinct lack of **T & C** in our leaders and those in power within the democracy that we enjoy in our political system as well as business structures generally. It is imperative that wherever possible such individuals communicate with us all in a **clear and specific manner.**

- Realise who you are, what makes you tick and crucially exists **under the body's bonnet** and so what is actually your make-up.

- Everyone is entitled to privacy and the enjoyment of confidentiality in their lives so we must guard against the insidious **toxic strands of journalism** taking further hold.

- Informality should not govern how we conduct ourselves all of the time and with all people, formality and tradition have their place in society. My two sons are both proud that I tell them **you are the only ones in the whole world who can legitimately call me dad.**

- Reality TV, rapid rise to fame, short-termism and altering our appearances seem to be all part of the **now society.**

- Short-termism with regard to our planet's resources, debt and lack of long-term strategic thinking has implications for the **family of the future world.**

- Preserve as much English culture as possible and celebrate our achievements, what defines being English and halt the disappearance of our traditional values. Bear in mind that **diversity exists all around us – there is no need to prescribe it.**

3. HEALTH & PERSONAL MAINTENANCE

LOOSEN UP OUT THERE!

Collectively, we should be clamouring for more relaxation in our lives and less stress which will eventually work through to fewer modern illnesses. Perhaps spreading work and jobs around the potential workforce can facilitate this objective, and people can all have weekends off (with obvious exceptions such as those working in essential services) ergo working less hours. Certain present day sicknesses, can be avoided altogether with small but fundamental alterations to our working habits. Stress can be reduced and even controlled – too much pressure is often applied externally by employers, schools, financial institutions and generally via other people's and our peers' expectations

A lot is heard today about the so called *"work – life balance"* and I wonder if we really have this properly in place. A host of science fiction films (which have a habit of being proved correct) show youthful looking individuals relaxing, exercising, and certainly not working as part of their living habits. I would venture to suggest that this is one prediction yet to come true and may not do so for decades to come. One particular American science fiction film called *"Solyent Green"* is highly apposite in this context.

Regular exercise has to form an intrinsic part of our lives. Each person in some way can attain better health with some degree of self-help. Allied to focusing on our fitness levels is taking more personal responsibility and moving away from the current blame culture which is so embedded in our society today. Walking, going up and down stairs, jogging, running as well as Yoga and Pilates are just some of the simpler, low cost and highly effective means to keep fit. You might wish to reflect on watching less TV, spending less money whilst in the **sitting position,** having less time in front of screens and providing fewer excuses for inaction. We can walk more, take up relatively inexpensive pastimes like swimming and cycling or do workouts at home using basic machines or just **chairs, stairs and yes, maybe we will attract stares!**

Unfortunately, for some people, due to ill-health, genetics and having hereditary conditions, it is difficult if not virtually impossible to derive any positive benefits out of exercising. The current economic climate meaning that certain people utilise almost all of their time earning a crust to keep the family financially afloat has to be borne in mind and I accept that, however desirable, such activity is not always feasible. For the vast majority of people with some effort and determination, a positive outcome will be seen within a short space of time.

I touch on the linkage of budget constraints and cuts in public services along with the availability of medical services elsewhere in this book. There have been positive developments in healthcare lately and these are to be highly commended. Automated External Defibrillators for certain types of life threatening cardiac conditions can be found in various public access units like train stations, airports, shopping centres and hotels. Another example are some specific National Health Service (NHS) GP Surgeries also known as Walk-In Centres (WiC's) located near to or actually in some train stations, which you can visit during working hours, and usually without making any prior appointment.

Along similar lines we now have NHS Walk In Centres WiC's in various locations meeting the needs of many people speedier and more cost-effectively than going to a main hospital. They supply a service providing treatment for minor ailments and injuries, with no requirement for a prior appointment and are open 365 days a year. These centres should be set up in many more towns and cities.

Despairingly, however, we have also witnessed in recent years a lack of access to healthcare that people should have within reasonable distances from their homes and timescales. Numerous GP Surgeries remain closed at weekends and evenings whilst for many practices up and down the country patients experience long waiting times to see a doctor at all. However documented, thousands of people wait weeks or months to see a medical specialist under the NHS and sometimes years before their treatment is completed. Avoiding serious medical problems and remaining healthy are not always just down to the patient!

IT'S THAT TIME OF THE YEAR

Our children should be accustomed to healthy habits from the earliest possible age in order to reduce the inexcusably high rate of child obesity in England (a modern day affliction rife also in many other countries). Good health is not a right but has to be acquired, and as always with children they will "learn by our example".

The NHS has a duty in my mind to cover the cost of regular medicals for their contributors – all who pay NIC. I advocate an **MOT (Ministry of Transport) FOR EACH PERSON** on this basis:-

- Once every 12 months for those aged 18 and over
- Twice a year for those aged 50 and over

- Three times a year for those aged 65 and over

Prevention of illnesses and diseases is surely a better and more cost effective method of handling medical care than the alternative for a lot of people comprising continuous medication, regular bouts of hospitalisation and surgery – EFFICIENCY IN PRACTICE! I champion unashamedly the motto *"prevention is better than cure"*. The whole panoply of treatment could be significantly reduced via the early detection of many major medical conditions and this also makes sound economic sense which will be music to the ears of health policy makers in the current financial environment. Reflect on the current situation outlined below:-

- It is mandatory to have MOT's for cars, buses and most vehicles on our roads.
- Regular checks are required for airplanes, ships and trains.
- A good deal of equipment has to be inspected at certain intervals of time - boilers, fire and safety apparatus, lifts and various electrical appliances.
- Consistent monitoring of the professionalism applies to many disciplines such as law, accountancy, medicine and the provision of advice on financial services.
- Periodic appraisals are undertaken for people in many jobs and types of work.

Contemplate who you know or know of (alive or no longer with us) that has a serious medical condition affecting their ability to work and lifestyle, where possible early detection could have helped, maybe even saved their lives.

Why not have ourselves checked out, be in the know and get in early!

In many cultures the expression *"as long as you have your health you are alright"* is quoted   but is this really taken to heart (the pun here is intended!). A lot of us devote little if any time to preserving ourselves and rather more in looking after material assets – car, house, electrical and household machines, clothes, computer gadgetry, not forgetting finances. We need a radical transformation in society whereby focus shifts to good habits that are beneficial to our minds and bodies, rather than in too many instances more harmful practices. I am referring here to smoking, taking drugs and the consumption of alcohol in each case to excess not where consumed in sensible quantities as part of socialising. This group of people, which is probably a sizeable minority, should contribute in some proportionate manner to the outlay involved in their treatment. Constant warnings and threats about the effects of these actions on health and in many cases to life itself seem to go unheeded.

A financial input to some extent from a person's earnings or savings can be made into a fund designated to cover some of the treatment costs, where it can be demonstrated that the ailment and consequent need for medical attention arises from "self-harm". I intend that such a stipulation only applies in severe cases where such actions have clearly led to a deterioration in health and requirement for prolonged medical care and where medical advice has been routinely ignored. I am aware of how contentious this would be, and having never smoked, taken drugs and only puffed a few cigarettes as a "rite of passage" in my school days, cannot know how difficult giving up an addiction can be. I do know, however, how treating people in these situations costs us all in terms of the public funds involved.

Being somebody who, like much of the population, has required the NHS during my lifetime are firm in the belief that some drastic decisions have to be made. I have felt aggrieved that the inevitable limited resources (monetary and medical) have been applied to people in the circumstances outlined above whilst being made to wait for appointments and treatment due at least in part to the burdening of the system by some undeserving cases being attended to and on occasions, given priority.

Anybody doubting my sincerity need look no further than a hospital A & E Department on Friday and Saturday nights, usually filled with any number of casualties who will come before you and be mainly responsible for the typical three to five hour wait to be seen. They may be bleeding, have broken, fractured or dislocated limbs, severe bruising and other motley forms of damage to their bodies following a fight or drunken brawl, or some other fracas which they cannot remember and invariably induced by excessive alcohol, drug taking or even worse. Some unfortunate folk are just caught in the middle attending hospital purely due to being innocent bystanders!

A culture of culpability needs to prevail as against blame and repeatedly being told that "we cannot do that because...". There must be a regime under which people do not expect somebody to always supply a remedy together with the provision of clear information on the outcome should they persist with what are expensive, unhygienic, dangerous and life threatening activities.

Increasingly the saying *"you cannot buy good health"* is out of date as the availability of new medical techniques and developments results in many people enjoying a cure for terrible diseases accompanied by the welcome removal of suffering for whole families. Obviously, this leads to issues such as the allocation and consequent prioritising of resources which will always apply unless we find an endless supply of money. As in many walks of life, controversial decisions need to be made by those at the top but instead of just fiscal considerations applying the moral, ethical and social features must be accounted for. Health is about more than just money, it is about the whole spectrum of issues and if some basic precepts are followed everyone will be **winners in the race for good health.**

ARE WE BONKING MAD?

Young people in particular still contracting sexually transmitted diseases (STD) reflects on many parties in our society and we all have a role to play here. I contend that parents have the primary duty to educate their offspring about such matters, preferably endorsed by what they learn in schools and information obtainable at any location where they might gather. STD is of course avoidable and a crucial aspect of how we look after and have respect for our own and other people's bodies.

SEX
Who Is There For You?

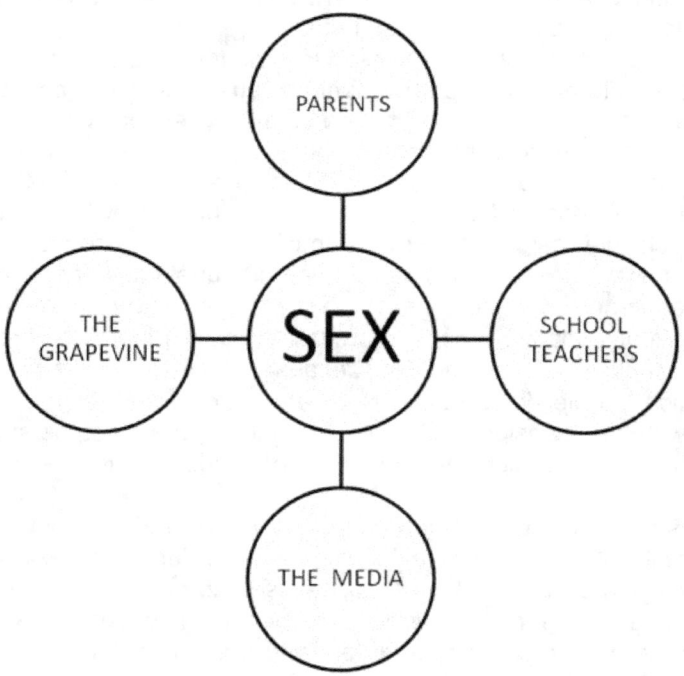

In our communities these days as compared to previous periods there exists more widespread recognition and knowledge of contraception, STD and of AIDS (Acquired Immune Deficiency Syndrome) apart from sexual intercourse itself. We will never prevent and should not seek to do so, adolescents being curious about and wanting to experiment with sexual orientated activities, let alone engaging in the sexual act which is the most primitive, powerful and basic human urge. The instinct for sex and reproduction has driven cultures, societies and much of our thinking since men and women first appeared on this planet. We can and should, however, make sure that our sons and daughters appreciate the need to have protected sex, the implications of leading a permissive lifestyle and have easy access to as many sources as possible supplying confidential advice.

More than ever in the past, peer pressure seems to yield an increasing crop of sexually active youngsters. **If you are active, be selective and protective!**

FOOD FOR THOUGHT

How often do we hear the expression *"you are what you eat"?* In many societies, like in England, great strides have been made in our staple diet together with the types of food and drinks now available in shops and supermarkets generally, so not confined to specialist outlets. The medical profession increasingly advises patients that small, but significant changes to their way of life, in particular the food and drink consumed, can improve many ailments. Dietary changes can also enhance everybody's chances of enjoying good health for the future and sustaining our bodies and minds for years if not decades to come. For a large section of the population poor and unhealthy eating habits persist and this needs to be rectified.

The appropriate foodstuffs and drinks are out there – in school meals, retail outlets, cafes and restaurants – but some of us need more willpower to make those healthy choices. The experts tell us that this does not mean always eating what we don't like, but building "healthy options" into our lifestyles whilst also appreciating the effects such choices can have on our teeth, internal organs, bones, and mental faculties. We can all make a large contribution to sustaining ourselves and not requiring medical resources unnecessarily. An element of accountability is at the core of personal well-being and down to all of us.

Health is arguably our most precious asset, what we predominantly worry about and the blessing of which we desperately want to bestow upon our children and loved ones. Many of us pray regularly and if asked would give anything for the gift of health which is viewed as beyond any monetary value. Plausibly, as discussed in the preceding paragraphs, we can affect and even to some degree instigate improvements to our current health by some basic changes to our lifestyles – worth a thought!

Do not ask what someBODY can do for you, but what you can do for your BODY

SYNOPSIS

- Consider whether there is any scope for you to achieve some form of or a better *"work-life balance"*. Reducing stress and the concomitant illnesses is to some extent within your power.

- The best medicine available which is inexpensive, widely accessible and recommended by all practitioners is REGULAR EXERCISE. Aim to spend less time in the **sitting position.** Even at home, try and become more active and think about **chairs, stairs and yes maybe we will attract stares!**

- Introduce an obligatory **MOT (Ministry of Transport) FOR EACH PERSON** aged 18 and over. This will represent an efficient investment into the nation's health so **why not have ourselves checked out, be in the know and get in early!**

- Where some medical conditions are self-induced hard and controversial decisions must be made regarding the costs of their treatment. Some element of personal monies can be applied to defray the expenditure involved so incorporating a degree of culpability.

- Sound health in this age taking account of the huge advances made in the medical field over the last few decades leads onto consideration of moral, ethical and social issues in conjunction with the allocation of financial resources. We must all be **winners in the race for good health.**

- As parents or anybody who has influence over our sons and daughters make sure that you impart to them the dictum **If you are active, be selective and protective!**

- We might like to consider what we eat and drink and put into our bodies on a regular basis and how it reacts to this input. Our health is to a large extent influenced by what and how much we choose to consume.

- The phrase which perhaps best sums up health is **Do not ask what someBODY can do for you, but what you can do for your BODY.**

4. FAMILY - WHERE WE BELONG

RELATIVITY – NOT THE EINSTEIN VERSION

Relax, we are not about to delve into the theories of this famous physicist and ask you to understand complex formulae and how they changed our understanding of the universe. Indeed, Einstein had a troubled life regarding family and his relatives and he is not alone there. The topic covered here is hopefully more comprehensible to us all or maybe not, our set of relatives!

This basic unit into which we are normally born, grow up, experience our most joyful times and memories, should underpin society as in all previous epochs and comprise both a mother and father being there. Sadly, this is not always the case in this modern era (and previous ones) and some of our most pressing problems emanate from lack of family surroundings. Dare I say that in some quarters, it has become fashionable or at least hardly objectionable to bring a child into the world as a single parent. I do acknowledge that this state of affairs is not always attributable to that parent (usually the female partner) with many other factors at play here.

Family constitutes the foundation of the world's major religions and civilizations and what many people credit with their successes and general well-being in life. The family is a pre-requisite for a balanced lifestyle which should be encouraged in all walks of life, as appropriate to our present age as in the past. Untold songs, films, historical events, breakthroughs in various fields, sporting successes and positive aspects of our world stem directly from the family.

Governments have a major role to play in this scenario by implementing tax policies favouring the family unit in addition to financially assisting less well-off people, to produce and raise children. Successive administrations in the UK, have enacted laws and put into practice measures which in fact have supported a framework of single people able to pay less tax, claim more for various allowances and a beneficial NIC regime in some cases, compared to being married.

OUR OFFSPRING AND THEIR LEGACY

Boys will be boys, girls should be allowed to be girls and children just children.

This obvious statement should be self-evident, bearing in mind:-

- The ever more sexualisation of our youngsters.
- Comparisons contained within school performance tables, and so leading to conclusions being drawn, for girls and boys at very young ages.
- Young children, in some families having to be carers for their parents in the absence of state assistance and unable to afford professional support.
- Products and services appropriate for adults being marketed to minors.
- Lack of local facilities for playing and exploring in parks and open spaces due to the legitimate and wholly understandable concerns of parents for their safety.
- The range of gadgets and home-based games which are operated from home.

All of these are instances of changes to how our children evolve today.

Covering family matters, parental responsibilities and child-related issues involve subjects for which there has never been available to date, and I doubt will be in the future, any professional course or qualification universally recognised as evidence of competency and success. I would venture to suggest that were such a programme to emerge, it would be fully indeed over subscribed many times. Nevertheless, I feel able to include some remarks on this topic here. Parents have a duty to bring up their children in the best possible manner compatible with their values and ideas taking account of how changes occur in society as a whole. The bulk of parents do an excellent job - many in the most arduous of circumstances.

Parenthood is no easy task and surely constitutes one of the hardest missions that we ever undertake during our lifetime. As a parent, father and individual member of society concerned to confront some current problems all around us, I wish to chronicle a few which are pertinent to this chapter and dealing with them.

Consider:-

- Making children aware and telling them it is unacceptable when they are rude or do unpleasant things in public such as spitting, picking their nose, throwing rubbish on the floor and putting their feet on seats.
- Encouraging them to *"mind your P's & Q's* Being polite is a hallmark of English Society and puts a smile on people's faces.

- Spend quality time with them playing, watching TV (yes this can be highly beneficial as they can ask you questions and you determine their tastes), playing interactive games to improve their reading, spelling and understanding of the world around us. Eating as many meals as possible together allowing for work and other commitments is a demonstration of such activity.

- As referred to above, let children grow up slowly as possible and properly compatible with what is reasonable and apposite to how we live in the 21st century. A conundrum, surely, which all parents all face. I would point out in this context:-

  a) Not encouraging or at least trying to dissuade girls to have pampering parties at too young an age, perhaps not before even entering their teens, let alone even prior to reaching puberty.

  b) Girls in particular at younger ages not dressing too provocatively when they are ill-equipped mentally to understand and deal with boys "coming onto them". This is a mute point, but I consider one that needs to be addressed. Doing whatever we can to avoid our daughters being viewed and worse still considering themselves as "sexual objects" has to be worthwhile.

  c) Explaining to them the devastating effects of too much alcohol and notably *"binge drinking"*.

  d) Inspire them to be bold and "**know when to say no**" to cigarettes, alcohol, drugs and especially sex.

There are no simple remedies and needless to say, to a degree these difficulties also relate to adults whose behaviour can be wanting, to say the least. I consider it imperative that attention is focused on the younger age-group. I want to emphasise that I do not view the overwhelming majority of young people in this light and stress that lot of our children and teenagers are a credit to society, their family and themselves.

Associated with this topic, I want to make a reference here to the circumstances in which children are born into the world. Teenagers sometimes turn into mums and dads thereby taking on the mantle of parenting and are consequently required to deal with the issues related to above or whatever will be relevant as to how their sons and daughters behave. There are numerous surveys and information available concerning the costs and responsibilities attendant on having children. My uncle once told me, although maybe this saying cannot be ascribed to him only, **children do not ask to be born.** My father-in-law always told me when I was dating his daughter "all in the right order please" and he was of course spot on.

Having children constitutes one of the greatest joys human beings can have and again the proverb *"it takes two to tango"* should always be called to mind when we are too quick to condemn either or both parties involved. We all bear personal responsibility for our actions. I mentioned in earlier pages, that since a men and women first appeared on our planet, sex as the most basic human urge has driven cultures, societies and much of our thinking. Why then is England continually it seems in recent times one of the Western European leaders for the number of teenage pregnancies occurring each year?

EDUCATING OUR CHILDREN

My premise is that school children should learn or at least recognise the wide variety of subjects which can be studied including: the sciences, history, geography, music, languages, the arts and culture, sport, the media and religions in order to fully appreciate the world and make informed choices about their future. They need to have a rounded education so as to have the best possible chance of making it today.

Learning about and most importantly taking part in sport is essential for children of all ages, sizes and outlooks on life so that children are aware of the significant benefits such as:-

- Improved health.
- Being competitive.
- Maintaining a suitable weight.
- Appreciating patriotism for sports people representing their country.
- Recognising failure and reward which are vital in all aspects of our lives.

Schools must have sports facilities with children becoming accustomed to the outdoors, physical exercise, and team spirit. Selling off fields to cut costs and over the top considerations of health and safety mitigate against this fundamental part of education leading to adults seeking attendances at gym's, keep fit classes and such like, which can be expensive and viewed with trepidation. Here surely, is one way that our country can continue to benefit from the London 2012 Olympic Games and other sporting successes achieved by our sports people in recent years.

Reward and failure are an integral tenet of life applicable not just in sports but with all subjects studied and tested. We should not conceal this notion from children but allow it's introduction at a suitable age as part of their preparation for life. Examinations are a basic element of education which they need to be familiar with, although I do not believe in their practice at too early an age. How often as parents have we heard our sons or daughters say "but dad that's not fair"! Our response is usually yes, the world is not fair knowing that what they really want is a more sympathetic retort. We know from our knowledge and experience that our children will be best served by learning the truth and it behoves us to implant this notion into their minds.

We are not all equal academically, physically, aesthetically, sexually or financially and this has always been the case throughout history. Infants recognise this and as they are reared through the early stages of life, some harsh realities become apparent within their family, amongst friends and people who they interact with. Diversity can be appreciated at an early age without having to be inculcated into us later in life and so often perceived as some sort of notion requiring the employment of specific people to promote, and seemingly endless bureaucracy to deal with the notion which is a "fact of life"

Money matters should be incorporated within the school curriculum and accorded much greater importance as a fundamental aspect of preparing for life, than applies at present. The rudiments of modern finance need to be ingrained in children at Secondary school as at present, along with sex education constituting the core for any syllabus applicable to children and adolescents, whilst accepting that both subjects are in tandem the preserve of parents who can make an invaluable input in these spheres. Political Science must also be part of the school curriculum, encouraging young people to engage with politics and help secure a higher percentage who actively participate in our democracy at general and local elections.

The turnout (the proportion of eligible voters who actually do vote) with regard to voting at a general election which is generally in the region of 60-80% and for young people (defined as between the ages of 18 - 24) it is usually below 40%! Consequently, by rough interpolation of these statistics, on average, just over 50% of people allowed actually exercise this valuable democratic right. In the past and even today, many wars are fought and blood shed so that individuals can have the benefits of a democracy and the right to elect a government of their choice.

Children are thankfully all born with differences and their education in terms of schools and universities should be according to ability and not political requirements. Educational establishments account for the formative years of our lives and those in authority are required to foster good habits and thoughts in our children. I consider that the vast majority of those involved in the provision of education to our children do a fine job and working in schools have to contend with ever changing curricular, occasional onslaughts from pupils and parental pressure in some cases not to mention trying to understand and deal with the children themselves. Political considerations also affect universities and other establishments of higher learning such as the prevailing level of student fees.

<u>SYNOPSIS</u>

- The family is the most suitable grouping within which to raise children and for all members to enjoy a balanced life - emphasised as such within most religions, cultures and surveys undertaken regarding human relationships. Government policies should promote this state of affairs, particularly in the fiscal field.

- In the light of how some of our offspring act and perceive the world today within what society and government deem acceptable however difficult our job as parents undoubtedly is, bear in mind that **Boys will be boys, girls should be allowed to be girls and children just children.**

- In that most demanding role of being parents we should seek to impress that it is indeed "cool" and for their benefit ultimately that they **know when to say no** with regard to cigarettes, alcohol, drugs and especially sex.

- Engaging in sex at young ages and teenage pregnancies are contentious topics but we still need to realise the responsibilities attendant on all involved when a new life starts – **children do not ask to be born.**

- All children deserve and should have access to a rounded education covering an extensive range of subjects to be adequately prepared for the workplace, forming relationships, becoming parents and life generally – which includes the concept of reward and failure.

- School curriculums must accord sufficient weighting to sports, money matters, sex education and political science.

- Children are born with differences and are not all equal which they become aware of at an early age in terms of their surroundings – to them diversity is a "fact of life".

5. THE STATE OF GOVERNMENT - TAKING CHARGE AND RESPONSIBILITY

"Power corrupts and absolute power corrupts absolutely"

TAKE ME TO YOUR CHIEF

There is a real dearth of quality leaders available at a time when they are sorely needed. Many parts of the world are experiencing a decline in moral standards, weighty economic problems, progressively widening disparity in wealth between rich and poor, overpopulation relative to estimated food and other resources and an ever increasing number of internecine disputes in various localities. Too many people in so called authority spend our time and money issuing sound bites and *"stating the bleedin obvious"*. They utter comments that anyone could, and which have no real impact in dealing with the issues at hand.

The United Nations (UN) and European Union (EU) to name just a few such bodies pass motions, send in observers and hold meetings but unfortunately, due to countries putting their own interests first, rarely is a consensus reached. At the time of writing the situation in Syria has been debated whilst China and Russia have applied a veto! We should evaluate as to whether the UN, EU and similar bodies really work and achieve their objectives, since they involve colossal expenditure. I recognise the valuable work these organisations undertake and successes achieved in a variety of fields and as a forum afford the means for many countries, large and small, to participate in programmes that are beneficial to people around the world. In the sphere of political settlements and wars, they are costly, unwieldy and all too frequently, fail to live up to their goals.

Even at national level the UK has hardly dealt meaningfully with certain key issues of the day. Like them or not such figures from history (some of whom are thankfully still alive today) including:- Margaret Thatcher, Ernest Bevin, Mahatma Ghandi, President John F Kennedy, Mother Theresa, Lech Walensea, Shimon Peres, Nelson Mandela, and many more, typify the sort of leaders we have had, acting as an inspiration to us all. You can no doubt name a lot more across the spectrum of human activity – where are people with their qualities today?

Our world urgently requires leaders with vision and the courage to confront the issues facing us, dispensing with the seeming endemic modern quirk of *"political correctness (known as being PC)"* that unduly influences what people seem to feel they can and cannot say. In my view it is not too dramatic to state that **our way of life is in danger of imploding** with nuclear weapons in the hands of a few countries that are led by autocratic rulers, the incessant rise in terrorism across the globe, overpopulation at an alarming rate in some countries and the rapid depletion of our planet's finite resources.

Religious leaders from all faiths have a duty to be more vociferous in defending the tenets of their religions and should also be less concerned about being PC. Adherents to a faith want guidance and a Rabbi, Priest, Mullah or whoever represents them must be bold and authoritative on the matters in question – homosexuality, poverty, exploitation of people, persecution and tyranny, abuses of the internet, the role of women, toleration of religious practices and instances in which government policies impact adversely on their faith. I appreciate that there are many different interpretations applicable to and even within each faith, but this must not distract those who have risen to a rank whereby they can steer the flock acting in a firm manner according to the faith's beliefs.

Who really controls the cost for public sector infrastructure projects, sentencing of convicted criminals, bears ultimate responsibility for victims of natural disasters and accidents via all modes of travel, accounts for mistakes made by the banks and other leading financial institutions together with the material which can be accessed on the internet? How often do we come across those who effectively *"pass the buck"* or should I say **pass the Euro**! by people that we expect to take decisions, implement suitable strategies and take responsibility for their actions. I have lost count of the occasions when no one person or body can be held accountable and finding this out is an absolute minefield.

We are normally let down woefully by these people who fail in their responsibility to take charge. Let us not forget that we are referring to individuals who have sought out these posts and a certain number of whom have employed dubious financial or other means to get there and devote considerable resources to staying put. Usually such people are well-educated, prosperous and worldly, so we justly expect them, and they have a duty, to deliver wherever possible. With high office comes high earnings and high expectations.

MAKING THIS KNOWN TO THE PUBLIC

Advertisements are frequently either misleading, inappropriate or both across the spectrum of goods and services involved, with regard to the intended audience at various times of the day. Examples to consider are young children and the elderly. We should not tolerate this state of affairs although there appears to be very little in the way of a deterrent or penalties applicable to wayward organisations, that perhaps have real teeth.

Another case in point of either unintended or deliberate deception is where a model or product shown is the more expensive version incorporating additional features at a cost, but where clearly and boldly we are told that "prices start from!" Airlines, railway franchises, coach operators and travel companies seem able to advertise the cost of a journey just one way? This is a new trend and you have to wonder why it is so popular. Since most people will need to purchase tickets for a return journey, the total outlay works out much higher for "a trip both ways" noting that coming back usually costs much more than for the outward bound voyage. To me, and I suspect many other people, this practice is solely designed to hoodwink consumers.

The general public as well as suppliers of such products and services are in need of direction and principles when it comes to their marketing. I am calling people's attention to the ban on advertising on TV and in cinemas that has been in force for many years now covering smoking and alcohol which are recognised forms of addiction whilst the promotion of gambling is permitted! At the time of developing material for this book, the Government was considering the advertising of abortion clinics and says that they would be tasteful! Abortion is a very sensitive subject and generally speaking frowned upon by the world's major religions and many cultures generally.

A basic flaw in our so called advanced society is the design and marketing of the products and services which are ever more complex, often with the intention of fooling people in their buying decisions by masking the true facts and figures. Consumers are confronted with excessive packaging which conceals the size of the actual contents. Are we really better served by an endless succession of sales initiatives like: Manager's specials, reductions only up until a specified date, winter/summer/spring/autumn and also mid-season sales, buy three items and get the fourth one free, get twelve months insurance and pay for only ten months in the first year and not forgetting one of the most popular – BOGOF! (buy one get one free). Retailers, wholesalers and suppliers generally must, however, be permitted to publicise their wares and maybe the dictum "caveat emptor" which is Latin for BUYER BEWARE, should be invoked more by the consumers. The power of advertising is well-known and of course why organisations pay huge sums of money to do so via all forms of media now available.

WHO SERVES WHO?

As a taxpaying citizen of this country, I would expect police stations to be open and staffed twenty four hours a day, seven days a week, fifty two weeks of the year as criminals commit crimes without prior warning and do not operate within set times. Despairingly this is not so, indeed some are only open set hours during weekdays whilst some local ones have been closed altogether. It is true that criminals do recognise bank holidays, festive periods and peak holiday times - as more profitable for them!

We need to ask ourselves what the point is of closures at specific times at night or during the day other than to aid criminals and make a mockery of providing a local service.   Similarly, there should be an examination of the case made for closures, reductions to and loss of other essential public services such as: GP surgeries, waste collections, library opening hours, and residential street lighting.

Banks and Building Societies need to ensure that their customers can do business early in the morning, late in the evening and on at least one day over the weekend. For people working normal daytime hours, it is not always possible to take time out and visit such premises during a brief coffee break or lunch hour – some do not even stop for anything other than going to the toilet. Many transactions can be undertaken online but there are cases, requiring attendance in person at a firm's premises so account must be taken of their availability.

My contention is that for plenty of service providers, it is in everybody's interests (employer, staff, customers and the government) to be open for more hours during a week – the benefits which I perceive are:-

1. Employees can work shifts meaning flexibility to accommodate their lifestyle and potentially more employees required.
2. Prospective increase in business undertaken which is attractive for the employer.

3. A wider range of customer needs can be met leading to their satisfaction and possible loyalty to that organisation.

4. The Government sees a reduction in unemployment and increase in their tax take.

Consideration should be given to abolishing the concept of unsocial hours since they are inherent in many jobs. We live in a *"twenty-four-seven"* society which I do not necessarily approve of, but accept that we cannot fully turn the clock back abandoning much of what is now part of our world today.

The sexualisation of children should not be permitted, but even when it does come to light, people seem slow to take any action. I watched on Channel 4 a programme called "The Sex Education Show" presented by

Anna Richardson, since during the fourth series in 2011 the issue of the sexualised clothing for young children was covered and she launched a campaign headed "Stop Pimping Our Kids". The programme brilliantly exposed some major retail transgressors. This programme illustrated how widespread the practice is for retailers to sell items which are clearly of a sexual nature. Individuals who are responsible for designing and marketing revealing underwear, thongs and other clothing primarily to pre and early teenage girls should reflect upon any daughters of their own – step back and think! Are these shops providing a response to what customers yearn for or discern an opportunity by creating a market and make money (which of course is their primary role) in a totally unseemly manner?

You may reflect on your own experiences where you really wondered if the organisation from which you bought a product or subscribed for a service exists to serve you as the customer, or it seemed to be the other way round! In a special investigation for the Channel 4 Dispatches programme on 15 January 2012, Richard Wilson was the presenter of "Richard Wilson on hold" and I was spellbound watching this. This broadcast explored the rise and rise of automated services across Britain, which highlighted the differences between these and manually obtaining train times, paying at supermarket for goods purchased and paying for car parking by putting money into a meter as compared to the automated alternatives available. This was a very illuminating programme, to say the least!

Masses of normally tranquil and law abiding people have come a cropper and turned into somebody unrecognisable only moments before when dealing with telephone help lines. In the event that you are able to press sufficient correct buttons on the telephone keypad and manage to reach the right department, have sufficient time and inclination for listening to the firm's choice of music whilst you wait and remember what you called about, the worst then happens. You are speaking with somebody who cannot speak good English, is following a prescribed menu and the dreaded "call centre" is clearly based overseas. You seem unable to convey what is required to the person at the other end of the telephone and may then be told to either contact a different department or go to their website for the information required.

On occasions, you may need to submit a complaint to an organisation – another potentially traumatic experience that can linger long in the memory. Letters can be issued to various people with no response forthcoming and as the customer, you become increasingly agitated. The initial issue confronting you is which individual or department you actually address the complaint to, especially in these days, of large conglomerations. I have also noticed that whilst many organisations require us to communicate by email, it can be difficult or impossible to obtain an email address for the complaint.

In the context of successive British Governments, there has been a proliferation of quangos (Quasi-Autonomous Non-Governmental Organisation) meaning one which is funded by taxpayers but not controlled by central government. Many are valuable and do good work but currently (as at October 2010), according to the Cabinet Office there were 742 such organisations in existence, and the present government was committed to axing 192 of them. A large number of these bodies are very expensive to run, produce little of any benefit to most people and continue operating for a long time during which they produce a string of reports and publications that make hardly any difference to our lives.

NEWCOMERS SETTLING INTO ENGLAND

Immigration must be carefully and sensitively managed in order to benefit everybody taking account of the resources required in these austere times thus avoiding a possible damaging antipathy towards anybody who chooses to come to this country. Many people arriving in England for the purpose of working or living do so legitimately, conferring advantages on themselves, their family and as a rule the country itself. Immigration is part of 21st Century life and should never be considered without the concomitant issue of emigration, as sundry talented and disaffected people leave our shores each year often resulting in the loss valuable expertise and of tax revenue the Treasury.

Some politicians on the far-right and far-left of their parties in the past and even in recent years have spoken in highly derogatory terms about this subject. I repudiate in the strongest possible terms such comments, theories and actions put forward by these people (or anybody else) since they are usually highly inflammatory and seek to cause division and incitement amongst the people of this country. Fascism and like minded racism, militarism are despicable with no place at all anywhere in the world. The proclamations made and solutions envisaged by admittedly a small but very influential number of people, are a portent of what may happen without a proper strategy devised and put into effect, since evil movements gain support and political ideas acceptance by playing upon the fears of people, however, ill founded they maybe.

Failure to acknowledge the potential impact of and clearly explain the benefits and rights relating to immigration will likely contribute to social unrest, economic burdens on taxpayers, and arguments across the political spectrum. The central theme of what some of these public figures and others propagate, and disturbingly find an increasing audience willing to listen to them, is an extreme consequence of unchecked immigration. Putting fear into people's minds, in view of the fact that a common thread applies to countries around the world involving residents, especially those without jobs, blaming immigration for their financial situation and many others for the general state of affairs in their homeland, is very worrying for us all. Immigration itself or any stated increase in numbers, is often touted as the sole or main reason for existing occupants' problems, which is false but takes hold rapidly in such circumstances.

The dilemma of how to integrate immigrants into society without generating misplaced resentment is a priority for all concerned, since a wholly unwelcome outcome of inaction will be the continuing rise in popularity of extreme political parties and fascist movements playing on people's fears which might lead, God forbid to even more electoral victories at local and national levels. Please note that *"history repeats itself"* a thought all should bear in mind. Our border control people, as far as possible, need to smooth out the immigration process and minimise the scope for delays and extra costs to be incurred.

In everybody's best interests, the speedy establishment of the right or otherwise to live and work in the UK should be the overriding priority to prevent people who arrive here from staying when it is illegal to do so and undesirable thoughts festering amongst some of the existing citizens. Those wishing to work and live in England, need to appreciate and be prepared for our culture, laws, tax and NIC system, social security benefits etc. The English way of life must be respected by those who wish to set up home in this country.

There have been instances reported in the media quite regularly concerning people coming to this country to work but without a proper command or even basic understanding of the English language and consequently, mistakes are made. There are of course, many instances, when immigration has been advantageous to this country. However unpalatable it may be, tens of thousands of job vacancies have been filled by people coming to this country (and this applies all over the world) which for whatever reasons(s), people living here did not apply for or wish to take up. Many people who choose to come to England, have a legitimate right based upon the days of the British Empire but as I have said, this needs to be established at the earliest opportunity by the UK Authorities so that they can go about their lives here with the proper documentation sorted out.

One point I wish to emphasise within the context of immigration and since we live in a multicultural society, is that people who are here have every right to be proud of and show their affection for England, English customs, English successes in any fields and stand up for their rights. People can feel and display loyalty to their own country as happens all over the world – being an Anglophile is a compliment and positive. We must not permit anybody or organisation preventing citizens demonstrating their pride in England on the spurious grounds of possibly offending some groups of people and trying to be too PC. This is wholly different from the vile outpourings of fascist orientated political parties and versions of extreme nationalism which are still around, some of which, gaining in popularity.

Patriotism is to be commended and does not equal racism but fascism does

EUROPE – WHO IS AT OUR HELM?

A recurring theme over the last few decades linked in with our social, economic and political way of life is who our ultimate legislature actually is. Directives, policies, dictums and overall law-making appear to emanate increasingly from this nebulous entity known as Europe. We cannot always determine who is really holding the reins of our government and effectively in the driving seat. Our parliament seems to progressively enact into UK Law whatever is handed down by the European Parliament and European Commission. UK citizens have a right to know who represents them as a government. Our political and business leaders are enjoined to consider Europe in terms of decision making even though England is a sovereign state.

Explicitly with Europe and the UK Economy, the precept should be *"no taxation without representation"* which was a slogan first used by the Reverend Jonathan Mayhew in a sermon in Boston in 1750. This motto summarises a primary source of grievance of the British Colonists located in the 13 colonies on the east coast of America and a major cause of the American Revolution (1775 - 1783). The slogan was also central to the cause of the English Civil War (1642 – 1651) as articulated by John Hampden who said *"what an English King has no right to demand, an English subject has a right to refuse"* in the Ship Money case of the 1630's.

In 2007 and 2008, as the world's financial markets came close to collapse and the UK economy as well as many other's the world over slid into recession, we needed leadership which was sadly wanting. We now receive regular bulletins about sovereign debt and downgrades of national debt across the EU and even some countries being close to bankruptcy. The blame culture seemed to permeate all communications from economists, political leaders, bankers and those deemed to be "in the know". Whatever was happening to our country's economy and financial system, we were told regularly was mainly down to external events, outside of this country's control! The message is the same one trotted out today and in recent years with gloomy forecasts, the remorseless decline of the Euro as a valuable currency and ever worsening trading conditions within Europe abound.

Despite European Summits, meetings of the International Monetary Fund (IMF), and countless gatherings of European Prime and Finance Ministers, no solutions have been found except to impose austerity measures on the populations of some European countries. Currently, for Greece the bureaucrats have concocted a series of national bail-outs each one incorporating ever more stringent terms and conditions. Spain, Portugal and Italy are also, on the so-called critical list when it comes to debt and likelihood of requiring a bail-out in the near future. In Europe, bail-outs are all the rage!

Many of us perceive an inevitable move to federalism and the apparent abandonment of this country's culture and traditions together with lack of control over our individual laws and infrastructure. Surely this bucks the trend for people to seek independence and self-government all over the world including people in territories within Europe. Our MP's and ministers should not talk about being in or out of Europe – we are part of the European continent geographically and there is no relevance to the terms pro or anti Europe rather we should be discussing being pro or anti European federalism or political union.

Undoubtedly fewer MP's are needed as European institutions progressively govern from their premises in Brussels or Strasbourg. Questions should be raised such as "what do you actually do?", "explain the meaning of your job title" and "what is your total remuneration package broken down by relevant sections?" of our politicians and ministers in Europe and the UK. Some of these individuals seem to have acquired now much longer names for their departments and functions, huge expense accounts and in a few cases – a whole entourage within their departments.

Many of the positive outcomes from European meetings – and I accept that some good does come out of these gatherings, could have come about in the normal manner by our UK based politicians and bureaucrats via ordinary meetings and long-distance communications with their counterparts in other European locations. There is no inherent requirement for any political union or extra layers of administration across Europe and we should all be mindful of the costs involved which devolve upon the already financially stretched citizens and taxpayers of each nation. Favourable benefits can emerge from pooling ideas and expertise - a normal business practice, whilst not necessitating countless people involved in a giant, unwieldy set-up which the European Union has become.

I suggest introducing a test which could be applied to people in various roles within government and public service providers, comprising an individual being asked "In your own words please explain in a maximum of two minutes what your job involves?". Alternatively, the question could be "How do you spend your working day?". This is especially pertinent to people who are said to work in Europe, as I explain above. The responses will be salutary for all concerned and I suggest, help rationalise the role of all individuals on the European payroll.

"IT IS HARD TO BELIEVE"

Political advice issued regularly by those in office here in the UK comprises banal statements like "please do not drive unless your journey is essential" and "please take extreme caution when visiting this or that location" but the Foreign Office is not advising travellers not to go there. What people need and expect from a government is much more precise information and assessment of any risks involved. Specifics and relevant data are required in situations where, quite rightly, a Minister or Secretary of State communicates via some form of medium to alert the public to some form of potential danger or harm.

Turning to political manifestos which are much discussed and debated at election time, what should we infer from their contents? Undoubtedly, the general public who politicians are meant to serve should be able to rely on what is set out in these publications and decide on whether to vote for a particular party based on the information as given! Rarely does a government minister or MP act on these policies or if they do, invariably they are a watered down or different versions apply when in office. In many cases, they are not implemented at all or just deferred. Frequently when in office the cry is that circumstances have changed, or the full facts and figures were not known by us at the time and that external factors are at play which are outside of our control.

The electorate cannot unrealistically expect to hold politicians to every statement of intent, policy put forward or even broad strategies which lets assume are genuinely intended at the time they are made. People can, however, and should be able to rely on the integrity of individuals and the party as a whole without wholesale U-turns throughout the period in office or just abandonment of what was said in opposition. **T & C** works both ways and politicians have a duty to fully appreciate how they take power in a democracy and not lose sight of this at all times.

There should be a mechanism whereby those in government are held accountable for the strategy and theories put forward and promised as against what is actually done, not just an opportunity every five years to have our say, and if we so choose - vote them out. Politicians need to possess the courage and ability to carry out as best they can the programmes which they set in motion. One example to illustrate this point relates to the provision of military assistance to a country or group of people then see it through.

In Libya during 2011 many who have expertise in the field of defence and ordinary people considered that there was a discernible need for "boots on the ground" rather than continuing with the simpler and less risky air strikes, but this was regularly ruled out by the government at the time.   We can also look at how the police in England confronted unprecedented, widespread riots and criminality in the summer of 2011, whilst lacking instant access to all of the appropriate force including water cannons and plastic bullets. Under certain conditions the possibility of bringing in the army was mentioned in the media and spoken about amongst the general public, but I understand that this could not happen instantly. Most important of all during those terrible few days, the police were considered to have lacked political direction. You cannot be in a position of power and government unless prepared to give true "leadership".

The Palace of Westminster (both the House of Commons and House of Lords) often look quite deserted during debates, which is more noticeable when a minister comes to the house to make a statement on a pressing issue of the day. Frequently the House of Lords looks almost devoid of attendees, with some who are there actually asleep! I find this quite astonishing and whilst would not expect either Chamber to be full all of the time, this is where our representatives are based and should spend much of their working day.

Are we "over governed" I muse. There seems to be an excess of ·legislation with innumerable laws impacting on everything we say, do and act upon. Can lawyers, let alone us ordinary mortals, be aware of and have any comprehension relating to the whole raft of regulations and rulings, let alone be expected to abide by them? I doubt this and also whether we actually need such a proliferation of decrees except to make some people's jobs seem valuable and life confusing for the majority of law-abiding citizens. Together with so much being added to the Statute Book every year, we have to contend with changes to existing laws, many a time that prove to be retrospective in effect, which are not always justified by events or required other than for political expediency.

For long-term issues like transport, education, energy projects, military undertakings, welfare provision, healthcare services and policing how can anybody have confidence in fully understanding what the situation is and will be in the future if frequent volte-faces are made for ostensibly politically motivated reasons. I propound that reductions to state benefits and constant changes to pensions are a couple of examples which I am familiar with, that are retrospective in their effect and mitigate against any form of long-term financial planning.

Difficulties abound for someone trying to look ahead when there is so much uncertainty about the future, which may be nothing new, but can almost certainly be combined with the knowledge that whilst it is reasonable to make decisions based upon present law and tax practice, the rules will probably be superseded by the time any plans come into force. My firm view is that any retrospective effects are unethical as well as financially detrimental. Somebody who reaches retirement, suffers incapacity, or loses their job at a future date might have made financial provision rightly assuming that present rules operate then.

People must feel empowered to save or invest for their own and family's futures and set up protection plans for life's unforeseen events in confidence that any changes made at a time to come will not adversely impact on their finances, otherwise why bother at all. I maintain that this also applies to state benefits which I know are funded on a pay as you go basis (if in fact really funded at all in this day and age).

During my time as a Financial Adviser, I dreaded informing long-standing, loyal clients that new tax provisions, alterations to pension rules or amendments to state benefits mean that decisions made in the past and monies committed to various financial arrangements will not work as foreseen. It comes as no surprise that the savings ratio in England has been declining, since amongst other reasons, people have little or maybe no faith in financial advice (not the Advisors but the process and products available) or even depositing money with banks and building societies. The people in power need to restore faith in the whole financial sector and a huge step can be taken making sure that the retrospective effects of changes made are minimised. Considering government policy over recent time, especially relating to tax, finance and benefits, it is axiomatic that goalposts will be moved, possibly several times! **Retrospection in legislation is simply wrong.**

EXCEPTIONS TO THE RULE!

All UK citizens, business entities and formal organisations of whatever sort should have the law uniformly applied to them. In many cases, this is not evident as shown below:-

- Why were Portsmouth Football Club still allowed to trade, since according to normal accounting and financial principles they were reported to have been insolvent? Deadlines to pay outstanding tax liabilities were extended on more than one occasion – a facility not permitted for others owing far less money to the Treasury.

- Why can people with substantial capital wealth place investments offshore with the sole or major objective of escaping UK Tax? I accept that tax avoidance is legal and tax evasion most definitely is not – which side of the line are such transactions really aiming at?

- Why, up until a very recent change in the law (squatting became a criminal offence on 31 August 2012), was it not possible to instantly remove squatters from properties, when it became clear that they possessed no ownership or occupational rights. The procedure has usually involved a timescale of weeks or months before the legal owners could resume their rightful residence again. No such rights accrue if an individual without the owner's permission sits in another person's car, moves into another individual's pre-booked seat in an auditorium or incurs expenditure on another individual's bank accounts.

- Why are MP's and government ministers when evidently guilty of claiming expenses beyond their entitlement, allowed to just pay the excess amount back with no other repercussions financial or otherwise? This line of reasoning does not apply to people who through a genuine mistake underpay some tax or NIC, maybe find themselves slightly in a negative balance with their bank or could be just seconds late using a parking space before the paid for time expires?

- Why following the banking and financial crises of 2008 that almost destroyed financial markets across the world, has nobody in the UK at the highest level within banks, the government, BoE, or the FSA been sacked without compensation and pension rights? Could people employed at all levels and in many different fields of work who are found to be responsible for such mayhem in their jobs, continue in their roles and suffer no consequences?

Try producing a short one page manifesto incorporating your own (and your partner's or family's) policies aimed at a potential electorate accurately describing what you would do in office.

People can be unequal under the law – like some who are wealthy, famous, or politicians.

GETTING OUT AND ABOUT

England is crying out for a fully cohesive transport policy incorporating road, rail, air and water-based travel. Long-suffering commuters, together with businesses, hard-pressed taxpayers and even tourists, are desperate for this densely populated island to move away from largely antiquated systems of travel. The government needs to facilitate cost-effective, reliable and straightforward journeys within and across towns, cities and across the country.

We are faced with endless debates around a third runway at Heathrow Airport or the construction of a new, third London Airport in the South East plus continued discussions and a huge time lag for High Speed 2 (HS2) to be completed. People encounter ever higher rail fares required for investment with promises of rail improvements measured in an increasing number of years, even decades along with the continued under-use of our canals and rivers for transport purposes.

Car owners and drivers feel under constant attack for daring to use a vehicle, variously being told that this mode of travel is not environmentally friendly, whilst enduring an expanding range of taxes on cars, fuel or both. Car owners also face a whole array of costs for just possessing let alone trying to park the vehicle – today we see all around us the condition which I call "**MMM…" Motorists Milked Mercilessly**. There does not seem to be much emphasis by government on road improvements with many trunk roads and motorways almost completely clogged up with traffic.

Whether stemming from Europe, the British Government or both, a proper strategy and funding arrangements need to be put in place with cross-party support as these projects usually take far longer to complete than the lifetime of any one government. Financing also must be clear and agreed upon well in advance if they are sustainable since frequently any transport schemes incorporate private as well as public funding.

Transport is an essential part of our lives now and a major factor in people's decisions on where to live whilst also a consideration for tourists visiting and people transacting business in the UK. More joined up thinking is a necessity so that wherever in England you happen to be, as far as possible, people can move seamlessly between road, rail, air and our waterways with enterprises co-ordinated to achieve maximum benefits with the minimum of disruption. Such an ambitious scheme will not be designed and implemented overnight and patently take decades to achieve results that we can see and enjoy but hey, with the political will to act, a start can be made and gradually become a reality.

"ORDER OUT OF CHAOS"

Law and order together with the criminal justice system in England to me is by and large in disarray, failing in it's delivery to the people who are to be served – you and I. Our legal structure is for the most part a poor reflection on those in power who should ensure that people feel safe in their homes, protected from those who break the law committing acts of violence against individuals and property not to mention properly punishing offenders and acting as a deterrent to others tempted towards unlawful activity. A competent legal regime is of paramount importance for society to operate successfully and has to be steadfastly upheld.

More prisons should be built and maybe use made of old decommissioned ships combined with uninhabited islands off our coasts – there has to be the capacity to protect law abiding people from criminals. Releasing prisoners early in their sentences, where despite protestations to the contrary from politicians, the underlying reason is patently the acute shortage of prisons, amounts to a recipe for disaster. The sentence passed must be fully applied and always suitable for the offence involved. Sentencing should not be dependent upon available accommodation or any economic related considerations. **Serious crime deserves serious sentences by serious judges – the S Factor.**

I recall numerous instances where the public have been outraged by the early release of prisoners which have included convicted murderers, rapists, burglars and fraudsters. Even accepting, as I do, the purpose of confinement and understand that incentives to reform and make amends for misdemeanours are incorporated within custodial sentences, a prime function of any democratically elected government is the protection of citizens with regard to law and order.

A topical illustration as to what a shambles our legal system is in combined with the negative ramifications of belonging to "Europe" is the case of Abu Qatada. Many sane individuals despair at how a legal system in this country and Europe, fails to deal with a case like this (by no means unique) and properly protect law abiding people, whilst a person known around the world to have been associated with and committed acts of terrorism is not serving any sentence for his crimes. We must be mindful that Britain played a key role in the creation of the Convention on Human Rights. Human rights has become a much maligned concept in recent years and almost a dirty term to use.

However amiable the intentions were for this treaty, to most people the human rights of the victims who are the aggrieved and innocent parties, have been superseded by those who abuse the rights of others and seem able to wiggle their way out of being held to account for their actions. This is clearly immoral and demands to be urgently rectified with the intention of restoring any semblance of faith in the legal machinations of European and British judicial institutions. Preservation of human rights, is in fact, a fundamental legal precept, enshrined in many of the world's major religions as well as systems of government, and quite rightly so. The bulk of the populations in countries throughout the world, I would contend, believe that the human rights of the individual or body that is wronged, supplant those of the guilty party.

Whilst certainly not the gravest of offences perhaps nothing highlights more the sheer hypocrisy of the current Coalition and indeed the previous New Labour Governments than the furore surrounding the MP's expenses scandal and paucity of criminal convictions which followed. Recalling this recent episode of financial shenanigans by our elected politicians and other instances where people who are famous, possess substantial wealth, in positions of power or indeed represent all three criterion leads me to suggest a novel offence to be incorporated within our legal system.

The concepts of tax avoidance (which is legal) and tax evasion (which is most certainly illegal) are often confused by people, either deliberately or otherwise and constitute the basis of much legal wrangling as well as underlying a lot of tax and financial planning by individuals and business entities. I am convinced that huge financial resources are devoted to and time spent by the legal profession and others on various actions taken and schemes set up with the sole purpose of "getting round or bending the law and rules in their favour".

Laws and rules exist for a purpose and in a democratic country have to be respected and observed. People should be deemed guilty of an illegal act and clear wrongdoing where they seek to subvert regulations. I can think of many examples where this behaviour is apparent just some of which are - investing large capital sums in tax havens and such like offshore jurisdictions, declaring bankruptcy and then setting up business often within a short timescale in another name or somebody else's ownership, sales people taking photographs clearly missing out less attractive features and misleading the buyer, making a statement or allegation which is knowingly prejudicial to someone and represents defamation of character and so then withdrawing it after the damage has been done.

We need to focus more upon people's motives than whether they just about keep within the law. I realise how debatable this idea is and relies on a person's intention, considering what a reasonable man would conclude and ultimately, rest on common sense applying. People always have and will continue to flout the law but since some have the means, power and authority to pursue a route to get round or bend the law, we should examine their actions closely and be open to what they are trying to do. Such individuals commonly accrue huge professional costs to achieve their objectives employing the top legal, financial and tax experts available and we must be vigilant since these people clearly know what they are doing and why.

Stone throwing and violence from children as young as 12 or in some cases eight years old during the recent riots in England left most people with feelings of anger and disgust that this happened in our country. Quite properly these actions were widely condemned – what about Palestinian children often even younger than this hurling stones and rocks at Israeli soldiers and even civilians! This does not attract the same criticism and is rarely mentioned in news media. What about child labour in many Asian and African countries, young women in England being forced into arranged marriages (against their wishes) according to some strains of Islam and other religious creeds! There are countless instances of such behaviour around the world that could be mentioned, let alone on our own doorstep which appears to proceed without necessarily attracting much attention or any criticism from people at large.

Turning now to the subject of girls and schools, I wish to highlight instances where common sense (as throughout the contents of this book) and somebody assuming control of a situation, are central to matters. I have read of cases where girls have been spending a lot of time during breaks and lunch hours applying make-up, against the school's policy. Also, examples have come to light where girls have been wearing skirts in an unbecoming manner. These are hardly new situations in today's times or necessarily in isolation particularly amoral. In some cases the parents have taken the side of their children leading to conflict with the school authorities whilst others have fully backed the teachers and staff in their actions.

Schools exist for the purpose of learning. A notable feature of the educational system is the long-established policy on wearing uniforms which should continue to operate, levelling out any monetary discrepancies between children from different backgrounds and family situations. Whilst being sensitive to girls (and boys for that matter) who are concerned to look good in the company of other people and feel confident about themselves, keeping clean, having clothes ironed and taking other reasonable measures to look respectable are sufficient for school days. Girls have always wanted to both look older and also copy their mothers – part of growing up. Both sexes have enough distractions in this modern world to contend with and the teaching staff ample issues requiring their attention, without having to allocate time for dealing with disputes about make-up, uniforms and such like.

Emphasis at these ages should be on serious studying and determining a career path, make-up and wearing any other choices of clothes is for outside of school and the best policy is for no make-up at all or any deviation from school uniform. There must be, as far as possible, order in the classroom and during school time. My wife informs me that when she was at school (up until the sixth form for ages 16 – 18), the rules were the skirt could not be rolled up under and hidden under the purse belt. No make-up or nail varnish was permitted at school and any violations of the rules was met with a call to the headmistress in charge of the girls which was a thoroughly intimidating experience and to be feared at all times. Parents would then weigh in with their two-penneth worth (no I am not that old but the saying fits perfectly).

Of course there are difficulties communicating with teenagers when at home or indeed anywhere, they are under peer pressure, this is the 21st Century and things are different to our day! Our children attend school during their most impressionable years and come face to face with many challenges all the time whilst their own bodies and thoughts are developing **hormones and moans!** Parents need wherever practical to support teachers and school staff in the very difficult job which they do in order that we can shape our youngsters into upright and productive adults. Children need to receive the same messages from all sources and put disputes about these and any other issues into a proper context.

You may conclude that having young and teenage children comply with what teachers, parents and even some of their peers say is grand but starry-eyed. For all we know nothing will change, but surely it is worth directing our efforts towards helping our children paying more attention to using their time wisely for their future benefit and appreciating how vital this is. Everything has it's time and place – we must all guide our youngsters to see this as clearly as possible.

<u>SYNOPSIS</u>

- The world seems to be without true, inspirational leaders who are really in the driving seat, dealing with the major issues of our time. A consequence is that **our way of life is in danger of imploding.**

- Who is now really accountable for their actions or utterances? I feel that too many political leaders play the game **pass the Euro.**

- Advertisements and promotions whilst obviously enticing, should at the same time be clear and accurate.

- What's the deal with Europe? Agreements on economic, legal and social and other issues common to member states is all very well and worthy but must always subject to the decision-making body(s) of each country's legislature. We ought to immediately dispense with the notion of any political alliance, move towards federalism and power residing with a top-heavy and largely unelected bureaucracy.

- Politicians owe a duty of to the electorate and all citizens of engendering **T & C**, taking a longer-term view on some matters and be held accountable for their policies.

- **Retrospection in legislation is simply wrong.** All governments must wake up to this and treat the electorate fairly who cannot be deemed to have the benefit of hindsight.

- The law has to be consistently applied right across the spectrum and be seen to do as much. **People can be unequal under the law – like some who are wealthy, famous or politicians.**

- Commuters, business, hard-pressed taxpayers and tourists require an integrated and cost-effective transport network to serve our towns, cities and countryside whilst also attracting businesses to our island. Governments of all hues have to eradicate a modern condition known as **MMM – MOTORISTS MILKED MERSILESSLY.**

- A widespread consensus exists amongst people in this country that law and order together with the criminal justice system is in a shambles, requiring a major overhaul. **Serious crimes deserve serious sentences by serious judges - the S Factor.**

- To deter individuals and organisations who are intent on bypassing existing laws, introduce an offence involving an intent to circumvent the law based upon some gain to them, by examining closely their motives and actions in pursuit of a particular endeavour.

- Common sense together with the exercise of authority are frequently in short supply in many walks of life. During school years, these two commodities must prevail where issues like make-up and school uniforms surface and we all need to handle our youngsters' **hormones and moans.**

Come to a decision on how you would treat, and if appropriate sentence, somebody in these situations:-

1) A newspaper journalist publishing false and incriminating information about a celebrity.
2) A youth aged 14 who assaults and seriously injures an 80 year old lady walking home from shopping.
3) A 32 year old mother of three children suspected of an intention to commit terrorist acts against civilians working in the City of London.
4) A middle- aged man who is found guilty of rape, for the third time in his life.

6. RELIGION IN THIS AGE – HAVING FAITH

NO PLACE FOR IT

Outdated, irrelevant and divisive are just a sample of the words and thoughts which many people today have about when asked about religion. The idea of a God is old fashioned, some people say and we now understand via scientific and other theories together with what has been proved, how we came about, exist, will leave this world combined with the universe itself. I have no intention of seeking to examine or provide any responses to these considerations which would deserve much more space than I wish to devote in this book and warrant the involvement of experts in these fields to fully deal with them. I do wish to state clearly my belief in God and religion which endures today, as relevant to the challenges which we all face just as much as in the past. I am also convinced that religion and science can and do co-exist.

During the Pope's visit here in 2010, he warned that Britain faced a threat from *"aggressive forms of secularism"*. In February 2012, Baroness Warsi who is the first female Muslim to serve in the cabinet being both a cabinet minister and Conservative Party Chairman went to the Vatican to effectively transmit the same message and told a training academy for papal diplomats that a *"militant secularisation is taking hold of our societies"*.

In an interview with the In Touch Magazine in the Autumn of 2011, the Chief Rabbi in the UK Lord Sacks said that in his humble opinion, the *"Judaeo-Christian ethic is the sole effective force capable of defeating the entropy which otherwise leads to the fall of civilisations"*. Lord Sacks also stated in a weekly pamphlet issued by the United Synagogue relating to the weekly portion of the Torah (the 5 books of Moses) in September 2011 *"A whole series of medical research projects has shown that faith, prayer and regular attendance at a house of worship actually have an effect on health and life expectancy"*.

We desperately need an infusion of core religious values forming the bedrock of how we live, our relationships with other people and the manner by which we define ourselves. For much of the time society seems to be bereft of structure and purpose whilst predominantly revolving around financial values and materialism. The principles and morals which in my view and those of many others, mankind should abide by, are incorporated within the three main monotheistic religions together with many other faiths.

There is certainly no place for the dreadful acts carried out in the name of religion over the aeons such as forced conversions, female circumcisions, mass murder, ethnic cleansing and the holocaust. Far too many wars have been started and fought in the name of God and religion with millions of lives lost and people suffering which sadly still persists today.

There is most definitely a place for tolerance amongst and within faiths wherever possible, and for religious leaders to stand back from making incendiary comments and observations that often just provide a boost to extremism together with the concomitant violence which follows, all taking hold. I fervently believe that the overwhelming majority of people who identify themselves with religion and observe the practices involved, do not endorse the radical actions of fanatics who unfortunately garner much publicity for their activities and disparage theirs' and all faiths.

WHAT IS THE POINT?

I propose that well established ethics and codes of behaviour which are embodied within the world's major beliefs, that underlie the policies of most democratic governments around the world, should be integral to our thoughts and actions. The absence of such standards, leads to low levels of satisfaction and morale often measuring our existence only by means of monetary resources. Financial considerations are progressively the order of the day further undermining a way of life embraced by the major creeds at least superficially adhered to by the majority of the world's population today.

I touched on this matter in the section referring to our behaviour and lifestyle. There is no need to look for or invent new codes of conduct in many cases today – they are already available and contained within well documented texts for religions across the globe. Morality, sexual behaviour, charity, political and legal systems, the family, health and medicinal issues, educational, economic, financial and environmental matters, forestry, natural resources, treatment of animals, employment practices and relations with other people - they are all there and covered.

Religious leaders need to speak out more about any threats impacting on their faiths – fundamentalism, homosexuality, the role of women, immoral behaviour, sexual abuse by those in authority and who should be trusted and many other current issues. The axiom to apply is "*Do not be afraid*". Religion and faith have a major role to play now as in the past and for the future. Our representatives in the wider world must pronounce on major issues affecting their creed providing a lead to members of that faith.

I perceive that society has swung too far the other way with regard to religious practices compared to past centuries. The ethics, practices, ideals, structure, framework and respect which are part of the world's foremost creeds, are badly missing in many cases. There is too much emphasis and even apparent worship of - materialism, superficiality, stars, public figures, instant successes, current fads and short-term ideas.

There was a debate taking place at the time of writing this book, about whether or not local council meetings should (as they have done for a long time) or should not include prayers. Some people who accept belonging to a particular religion and atheists, maintain that saying prayers is inappropriate. When disasters happen (natural or man-made) most people think or talk about saying prayers and coming together and religious leaders usually come to the fore, and their pastoral work is highly valued.

In the dreadful episodes where people (even young children) just disappear, we regularly witness people in a town or village gathering around a local place of worship to receive and provide support and the religious minister is called upon or just volunteer's to pronounce soothing and comforting words for the occasion. In many films, a priest, rabbi or mullah utters key lines as part of the script, regularly striking exactly the right note and showing a great understanding of what is happening.

Most of the world's nations have a state religion and known as a Christian, Muslim or Catholic Country. In the USA, every session of Congress where in fact there is a clear separation of church and state, starts with prayers. Recently Lord Sacks opened Congress and his prayer was broadcast on both sides of the Atlantic. Religion is part of many people's lives and arguably should form part of a child's education at an early age. This does not mean that no room exists for a difference in opinion and practice so that everyone can decide to what extent, if at all, they follow a religion.

Parents might wish to consider instilling the virtues of religion, along with issues such as sex, politics, finance and many other aspects of our lives into them to what extent they deem it appropriate to do so. The basics of religion and these other subjects can assist our children to grow up as "fully rounded" as possible where they are addressed by those who are normally best suited to the task – parents.

CONTROVERSY IS ACCEPTABLE

RELIGION, SEX AND POLITICS the so-called subjects to avoid in polite, social conversation, comedy and other forms of communication is a concept that many of us have grown up with. Without these topics, what would we talk about and laugh at! Much comedy is based on these three themes whilst people from various walks of life often express doubt as to whether the humour is within acceptable bounds of taste and that in itself might lead to heated debates. People can nevertheless have differing views on many contentious issues but this does not mean we that should all embrace deviations from what may be deemed the norm or acceptable by our families and society as a whole. The "silent majority" must be heard and understood as well as those who hold alternative views on religion and life in general. Children in particular but not exclusively, need a foundation for their existence so abiding by a religion as referred to above, being heterosexual, believing in the policies of a political party are all conventional and should not be discarded just because we must all be modern!

I would stress, however, that people who do hold contrasting notions must be heard and not prosecuted for their views. Throughout history individuals have adopted different stances on a whole range of issues and tolerance is vital for humanity to survive. Many people chose to be identified by their religious convictions possibly ahead of their job or any other role in society. I would suggest that many faiths and creeds have more in common than we often think is the case. Plenty of worthy people cite religious beliefs as fundamental to how they lead their lives and even keeping them on the" *straight and narrow"*.

Too many people, in my experience, cite religion as the catalyst for conflicts, intolerance plus holding back progress on some fronts like contraception and homosexuality. Religion has negative connotations and deemed not to really be part of 21st Century life for large sections of the population, seeming to be peddling archaic ideas and interpretations unrelated to modern day issues. I beg to differ, as explained above and urge a rational approach to faiths and what they mean.

Restoring religious values to at least part of our learning, thought processes and day-to- day activities, will be a major contribution to building a sound society and alleviate some of the problems that we all face. Indeed, solutions to our difficulties are there, relevant to as much of our contemporary way of life as when they were initially applied to situations then current. People are seeking parameters and leadership as never before in this highly materialistic, fast moving and complex society – religion is there for them.

<u>SYNOPSIS</u>

- The world's three monotheistic faiths – Judaism, Christianity and Islam together with many others followed by people all over the world incorporate standards of ethics and morality and an overall framework applicable to society today as in previous epochs. We have no need to always seek the implementation of a new code of conduct – much of it is all there for us.

- Religious values can and do combat the prevalent low levels of morale and satisfaction with our lot along with financial values, materialism and the general secularisation of recent times. Look them up, you might be surprised at the findings.

- Religion is a force for good and positive aspect of so many people's lives. Wars and acts of violence committed solely in the name of a religion and constituting blatant aggression alongside some conventions is abhorrent with no place in society. Extremism is to be confronted as much as possible. I am aware and accept that much blood shed occurs in self-defence.

- Our religious leaders must speak up and out on essential issues affecting their faith to maintain credibility as spokespeople for that faith.

- Children ought to be made aware of their family's religious heritage and learn to appreciate the features of other faiths that people follow as part of a rounded education.

- Religious convictions are credited by many people with keeping them on the "*straight and narrow*" and so the merits of systems of worship based upon a belief in God. We should not allow the harmful and distasteful practices some people ascribe to religion disproportionate publicity.

7. A ROLE FOR EACH PERSON – ROOTING THS OUT

All of us combined should recognise what we do have that is not necessarily money-related or consumer-driven focusing upon what we can appreciate. Some examples to contemplate are:-

- The five senses (sight, smell, touch, taste and hearing). How many are we blessed with and enjoy full use of?

- Modern sanitary conditions, only too apparent upon seeing the awful, distressing sight of millions of infants let alone people generally, without access to clean water and so prone to various diseases and death.

- A wide range of hobbies and forms of entertainment to choose from which can be enjoyed indoors, outdoors, maybe passive or participative, old, modern, suitable for the young, middle-aged and more senior.

- A tremendous number of different subjects now available to study at school, universities and remotely at all ages and various mediums by which we can learn and increase our knowledge.

- Living in a country which is:-

  a) One of the world's oldest democracies.
  b) Tolerant of religions and their practices.
  c) Possesses an enormous diversity of landscapes, historical and other sites of interest not to mention climatic conditions.
  d) Boasts an international language spoken throughout the world.

Every one of us is unique with our own functions to perform, place in the family and society as a whole. We should undertake a **personal audit** and spend some time on introspection.

GET A LIFE

Following the advice of a Rabbi at my local synagogue I became aware that, if not obvious to me beforehand, happiness is the key to life and good health. A state of contentment and well-being involves gratitude for our environment and the world around us. We cannot always smile, look jolly and have no cares at all - but there are surely some positives we can recognise. I believe that everyone can identify aspects of their lives which are negative and these in turn more often than not, constitute the focus of how we conduct ourselves. I accept and indeed agree that money is a vital requirement of a satisfactory existence but should never be the SOLE ARBITER.

My eldest son is convinced that each person is put on earth to perform a role and it is merely a matter of time before we individually determine what this is. He derives this notion via the spirituality and religious observance embedded in his life - in time I have come to recognise and partially share this view especially since the medical condition that I live with has altered my fate. We have distinct attributes all of which are appropriate for mankind to exist and develop. Lack of money and good health, to name two of the leading facets of life are major drawbacks to achieving contentment and cannot just be dismissed. I regard family, stable relationships, religion or spirituality, good and enduring friendships, an ability to put matters into perspective, cognizance of those worse off than ourselves plus a positive outlook on life right up there in determining our position on the scale of happiness. Plenty of people lead a positive lifestyle and are sometimes great examples to us all.

My late father was a man of great wisdom always pointing out that when introduced to somebody for the first time, or when people appear on a TV show after learning of their name the next piece of information sought is their occupation! This inquiry, when answered, seems to govern in our minds the sort of person that they are. Human beings do not necessarily have a calling to be a bus driver, accountant, policeman, electrician, chef, IT Specialist, marketing director and so on. People take up jobs, enter into professions, follow a vocation or go into a particular type of business – regardless of how described, they represent a means to derive earnings so enabling them to provide for their financial needs. Some of and may I venture to suggest fortunate people, do aspire to a particular line of work early on in life for whatever reason.

Who we actually are and what we represent is not governed just or in the main by how we earn our living. People are part of a family, pursue diverse interests, enjoy varying states of health, are an integral part of past events, demonstrate assorted achievements in life, have different outlooks and most importantly are distinctive. There are plenty more characteristics and elements which define our individual "self". Everybody has a role to play, even if not immediately evident or in an immediately recognised form.

"BEING SATISFIED"

I maintain that nobody does or maybe will have everything that they wish for. In this context, I have ruminated upon the many facets of our being alive – health, wealth, children, where we live, the work which we do, pastimes that we pursue and our family structure as a few examples. We read or hear about people who seem to have had the odds stacked against them and for a brief period of time, appear able to reflect on how fortunate we actually are. Most of us in this country during the course of our lives do not encounter natural disasters, famine, civil war, children dying in early childhood, lack of water and washing facilities, extreme cold and hot weather (on a regular basis) and shortages of the basic ingredients for our way of life.

Undoubtedly, as I have already stated, some individuals are blessed with good luck (but also work very hard) to attain income from their chosen careers like sports people, professors of various disciplines and entertainers. Clearly these people do get satisfaction from their work as well as usually being handsomely rewarded financially. Some of us win substantial sums of money or receive large inheritances, have jobs which take us to different parts of the world, are able to have children and in turn grandchildren or live in desirable parts of the country. Certain people do, therefore, get a lot of satisfaction in different ways and at different stages of their lives.

Many people regrettably, however, lack those dimensions to their lives which they dream of, others have experienced or are still undergoing - unhappy marriages and relationships, lack of money, live in poor and even dangerous neighbourhoods, illness preventing travel or participation in many activities, unable to obtain a job, been made redundant, are subject to either mental or physical abuse (or both) in their childhood and infertility. Lifestyle events mould us and wherever possible, let us be grateful for what we do have.

The general public do not need to continually hear "what can England do for young Muslims?" or indeed any other ethnic group. There are numerous instances where young Asians, Jews, Blacks and people of all backgrounds make their way in life unhindered by state authorities and despite representing what is often called an "ethnic minority". Indeed many people, who are legally eligible to do so, come and settle in England since they have better opportunities than the country where they presently live or are the descendants of those who came to this country in the past, as I comment below. I concede that despite the best efforts of people involved with race relations and the multicultural society that is now England (and of course many other countries) people do run into discrimination in many fields and feel understandably disadvantaged.

Perhaps a thought – for me, more than likely for many of you also, it is both uncomfortable and reprehensible that homosexuals, women, those deemed to be disabled together with young people entering the jobs market without much work experience and people deemed to be advanced in years also seem to be at a disadvantage in society today. The same situation applies in many other parts of the world. I do not condone this state of affairs and maybe humanity will in time to come recognise the role that everyone can play in our world. Striving to achieve our ambitions with whatever we have been endowed with, appreciating the innate abilities that we possess and taking stock of ourselves generally, I suggest are a recipe for at least moving towards self-fulfilment.

People of all races, colours and ethnic groupings should not be able to settle in England (or in my opinion anywhere else) without a valid reason and legal entitlement to do so as recognised by English and where appropriate international conventions. Moreover, people ineligible to enter our shores must not expect to enjoy and specifically receive any form of immediate or preferential right to jobs, a particular standard of living, state benefits, housing, plus further financial aid and services that are available to the indigenous inhabitants via payment of their taxes and NIC. I do not include here people who are legally eligible to be in England and as per recognised international rules seek asylum here. Nobody who manages to enter England via the sea ports, airports, train termini or any other gateway, should be afforded access to resources that have to be financed by somebody which means the taxpayers on a long-term basis unless they have the right to do so.

There are millions of people around the world who do not have fulfilling lives according to their own criterion and eager to leave where they are now and head to another country and it seems that England is high up on or top of that list. There are often dubious grounds for their desires which can be anything from having a criminal record, debts built up, family disputes, unemployment through to general dissatisfaction with what is happening in their native land. England has to balance a sympathetic approach to those who wish to lawfully come here and a firm line with individuals who can only be said to be "trying it on".

We must avoid encouraging divisions and resentment amongst English citizens and facilitate their satisfaction when dealing with this highly sensitive issue. Once established in England, and again I would contend any other country, it is incumbent on each of us to determine our capabilities and how we can function to the well-being of all concerned. Vitally, however, those coming to England ought to make all possible efforts with a view to integrating into the culture, learn the language and comply with the laws of the land whilst never losing sight of and practising their individual traditions and way of life.

I firmly believe, however, and urge England like all other nations of the world, to be conscious of and explain clearly irrespective of party political dogma to the population, the country's obligations to those who we may describe as foreigners but do possess rights to make a home in this country. In conjunction with how immigration is dealt with, countless people who currently reside in different places all over the world, are entitled to live in

England and perform their role in the world into which they have been born. For historical and many other reasons, they currently live elsewhere and will only fulfil their purpose in life once established in the right place leading to everyone's satisfaction.

THE UNIFORM APPROACH

WE ARE NOT ALL EQUAL a bold statement containing a fundamental truth that must be grasped – let us take a positive rather than negative stance on this matter. Humankind comprises a huge variety of characteristics, religious observances and general orientations. Discrimination in any form is completely unacceptable and outlawed - many countries, like our own, thankfully have in force legislation to this effect which was long-overdue but nonetheless very welcome.

Individuals cannot always be compared to others or a particular template, since this has adverse implications for employment, housing, the provision of healthcare, legal systems, dress codes and financial matters. To what extent, I consider, is it right that somebody of a particular persuasion expects the people around them irrespective of the locality, to abide by that person's way of life. Correspondingly, should any one person be forced to accept the conventions and behaviour of those around them who are frequently in the majority?

These are but a few of the inferences stemming from any part of our planet in which the damaging policy of EQUALITY is foisted upon it's populace. Societies need to accept that the often maligned concept of "diversity" is standard in terms of how human beings were created. Our world can attest to the disadvantage of millions of individuals being forced to adopt a consistent and unchanging way of living – communism and extreme forms of socialism, repressed people in many states under totalitarian regimes and slavery which whilst abolished still flourishes in an economic or social format, let alone physically and mentally in many parts of the world.

In England the concept of equality manifests itself via league tables for schools, medical tests based on a system of points accrued, applying human rights practices to all irrespective of their actions and striving to adopt and enact rules emanating from Europe which apply to all other member countries. Growing up and living in a world where equality is applied to the detriment of any particular society runs counter to what is best for us to perform our role in that environment. We can even see this happening on a micro scale in terms of different regions of the UK – Yorkshire folk, Lancashire folk, Northerners and Southern softies, large towns and cities compared to smaller municipalities and villages are just some examples.

LET'S TALK ABOUT SEX

Men and women are NOT EQUAL there I have said it now, and likely brought upon myself howls of anger. Personally, I thank God for this as we should recognise, celebrate and generally seek to understand (if we ever can!) the distinguishing features between us. Much of our history and cultures is foundered upon these key differences – appearance and physical features, mannerisms, clothing, life expectancy, instincts and overall outlook on life. Only the female gender can produce children and consequently bear a much greater burden throughout their pregnancy and of course the birth itself compared to their male counterparts. The ability to actually physically produce a child inherent in the female sex governs much more than the issues which many of us talk and if brave enough, joke about. Reproduction could not happen if equality existed.

None of these remarks detract from my firm belief that women should not suffer different treatment to men when performing the same job, enjoying access to various facilities, age criteria, entitlements under the law and in many other spheres – in other words discrimination purely on account of their sex. I realise that women have had to fight hard for such rights and innumerable remain indignant that they had to take any action at all and still have to in some instances. Both sexes should have full parity wherever proper and apt for the situations involved – being born female should not be a hindrance in life. Clearly, though, society must acknowledge circumstances in which differences are relevant such as bodily functions, the need for privacy in public conveniences, nature of discussions and approach to "dating and mating", sensitivities to appearance, weight and age, religious and cultural distinctions together with many other slants on life. Differences does not mean disadvantages.

A particularly horrendous contrast in the behaviour towards women, by unscrupulous men which has no place in our world, that should be condemned and attract the severest of punishments, are rape and sexual assaults. These crimes usually scar women both mentally and physically for life. An additional disparity as to how in general men act towards women concerns the working environment, since even now, a lot of females suffer silently from various types of sexual harassment. A good example of "the boot being on the other foot" can be found in the 1980 American Comedy Film "*9 to 5* " - **a real treat for women, but please do not try this at home or in your workplace!**

I assert that women should enjoy different treatment to men where relevant. The separate features applicable to each sex is a lesson that we have to learn in many situations. Consider for a moment the relationship between and actions of - brothers and sisters, husbands and wives (some of us are still learning here!), dancing partner's roles, singing ranges, maternity issues, medical conditions, sporting rules and not to be forgotten sexual intercourse. **Diversity of the sexes** should be celebrated.

The title of a modern, international bestselling book in the 1990's written by an American author and relationship counsellor John Gray about relationships between men and women "Men are from Mars Women are from Venus" has become part of popular culture and a well-known metaphor.

THE FACTS OF LIFE

The breakdown in the family unit, some parents no longer taking on the mantle of being proactive in discussing this matter with their children and the pervasive liberal attitudes to promiscuity amongst some sections of the community have all led to how some people treat sexual intercourse. The safety and development of our offspring until age 18 is predominantly a parent's responsibility under English law. We should abhor and refuse to countenance young and frequently vulnerable girls becoming pregnant at all, not least under the circumstances where routinely the boys involved disappear into thin air.

Underage sex (the age of consent is 16) is illegal in England and the relevant parties should be forced to deal with the consequences of their actions. One financial ramification of this situation might be to withhold the allocation of state benefits to any party until the parent(s) have been identified and, wherever possible, held accountable for their children's actions. Alternatively the law should make it mandatory for the father or his parents to make a financial contribution towards the upkeep of his child up to a specified age.

I acknowledge the tremendous difficulties there would be in implementing such measures and time this would take up not least for the police and other people involved in law and order. Admittedly, young people who are not even teenagers or in their early teens, predominantly lack the mental capability of dealing with the aftermath of the sex act. Notwithstanding, the cornerstone of a society in which as far as possible children are brought into the world in a loving, family environment must be where individuals recognise and do not abdicate their roles. The high rates of pubescent and generally unwanted pregnancies amongst young teenagers is disgraceful and we need deeds not just platitudes.

Young people who are referred to as "sexually active" and their parents might like to reflect on the high ratio of couples (I understand that it is in the region of 1 in 10) where one or both parties are infertile and would do anything to produce a child. Even resorting to In-Vitro fertilizations (IVF) is not always successful and very expensive. Reproduction is one, if not the main areas in which we differ from animals – humans are capable of making choices.

SEX - THE WHOLE PICTURE

- Legal Age
- Contraception

- S.T.D (Sexually Transmitted Disease)
- Peer Pressure

- Virginity - A big deal
- Having a Child

- A Parent's Role
- Upbringing Costs

- **YOUR CHILD FOREVER**

We should all contemplate how it often seems to be that commonplace nudity, lewd activities not to mention swearing, excessive drinking and drug-taking together with the accompanying rowdy behaviour partly contributes to our perspective on sex and social conduct, in particular how all of this is portrayed in the media. Everybody has a role to play here – it is not just a simple matter of blaming other people! Many programmes on TV, advertisements, newspapers, shop windows and some film trailers (even when stated as suitable for an age category) can be unnecessarily suggestive and focus on these potentially unwholesome aspects of life.

I do not consider myself to be prude or that anybody else should be censored as to what they view or indulge in. I am happy to enjoy what is deemed to be a "dirty joke", feel it perfectly acceptable for those who have reached the age of majority to make their own decisions about what material they read, look at and enjoy whilst believing it right and proper that sexual matters are in the open. I take pleasure in seeing the humorous side of contrasts between the genders (how boring life might be without this pastime!). Naturally, I also recognise that in every generation, all of us need to deal with and be sensitive to puberty whilst meeting the challenges of openly discussing, reading about and for many people delighting in leading an active sex life. The facts are that, however old-fashioned this might appear to be, parents need to engage with their children about sex and it's implications, counter the many myths which abound in the world regarding sex and provide a good family environment within which any sexual-related issue is considered.

BEING OLD IS BETTER THAN THE ALTERNATIVE!

I have already alluded to my father's philosophy on life and the above comment was one of his most significant observations which he repeated during the later years we had him with us when asked about his health. He died just a few years ago aged 82 but clearly recognised the merit of reaching an old age and like others of his generation, some of who gladly are still alive today, never expected to live into their 70's let alone 80's. Being advanced in years, is a positive aspect of how humanity has developed in the last few decades and is to be admired.

What is commonly referred to as "ageism" is another demonstration of how some people   act towards and perceive those individuals who live past the biblical "*threescore years and ten*" and a form of discrimination. Everyone whatever their age has a role to play and is part of society. Discarding TV presenters, actors and those in the public eye on account of age is unethical and wastes the most precious of all resources – THE HUMAN ONES!.

Currently, there is too much emphasis on and credence attached to looks, fashion and the superficial aspects of products and services. Sadly, in many ways this approach applies to people as well. An obsession with youth and beauty as defined by certain individuals in the media, hinders and often destroys a person's enjoyment of life, participation in employment and undertaking tasks which they are ideally suited for.

Becoming old is a natural and an integral part of our existence that will be more pertinent in the future as life expectancy increases exponentially. A modern term is most fitting to use here "let's get real" as this group of people are here to stay and for much longer in the time to come. We need to embrace on our TV screens, in films, singing and dancing in fact for all forms of entertainment those in their "third age" or also called "silver surfers". The 1976 Science Fiction film "*Logan's Run*" deals with these themes in a chilling way.

A timely reminder here, if one is needed, that the older age group have a very high turnout rate and are keen to exercise their democratic right of voting in General and Local Elections and usually in accordance with the values that they grew up with. Reportedly, they also have the financial muscle of significant spending power and needless to say the time to shop around for their purchases.

Consider the roles played by a whole assortment of people like Bruce Forsyth, Meryl Streep, Clint Eastwood, Richard Attenborough, David Attenborough, Tony Bennett, Tom Jones, Barbara Streisand, Tony Benn, Dames Helen Mirren and Maggie Smith, Ronnie Corbett, Trevor McDonald, Bill Kenwright, and so on. Maturity, experience, wisdom and different perspectives accompany us as we age with everyone benefiting from the role elder people play in our community. In these so called enlightened times, we must not marginalise this ever increasing group of people who have much to offer us, having lived through countless events and happenings, with first hand experience, that we can only read about in history – **they are part of our history.**

It would be interesting for you to think about and jot down how many famous people who are still active in public life or their specific fields (like entertainment) who are aged 65 or over, 75 or over and even 90 plus!

Older people who are in some way infirm and consequently not able to fully participate in society, might wish to consider how CHARITABLE are we? My youngest son recalls an incident which happened on a London underground train during one of the "Tube Time Challenges" the family was involved in many years ago now, which was a world record attempt to visit all London Underground Stations under certain conditions to gain an entry into the Guinness Book of Records and served to raise money for charity. Whilst walking up and down the carriages with a collection box, he was confronted by a seated passenger who took him quite by surprise. My son was told to the effect that never mind collecting for children, what about old people?

Participating in a virtuous activity as raising money for underprivileged children, he could not understand why somebody would make such comments, and at the time, neither did I. However, as I reflect on this comment and how our elderly are treated, this does make some sense to me now. Most of us cannot fail to be touched by images of children starving, having been abused, living with a disability and generally in some way being different from normal, healthy babies and infants. Do images of those in their "golden years" inspire similar thoughts and desire to financially help out as for children?

There are numerous encouraging instances where we have assisted the elder members of our society such as medical and lifestyle appliances being modified, internet and online shopping, reduced entry costs for many public attractions and facilities plus a whole range of activities offered by public bodies and private organisations. Such developments also help people who are disabled and much younger in addition to their older counterparts.

Many religions and cultures focus heavily upon looking after the elderly and respecting them on account of their age and longevity. Politicians place, at least in theory, the welfare of our elders and long-term care high up on the political agenda. I once read a very fitting quote that "*a society is judged by how it deals with the elderly".*

People in some parts of the world will live for much longer than in recent decades, and I am not sure that we are prepared for this in terms of healthcare provision, pension planning, recreational activities, charitable work and so on. I have referred to some examples where perhaps there have been changes and positive approaches adopted, but these possibly only tackle the surface. I do not believe that we have grasped the enormity of the situation combined with the impact on resources, the general population and government policies.

Young, middle-aged and the elderly – how should we define these age groups? Can we be sure that car insurance policies for the "over 50's" and free bus passes and other public services for the over 60's or even 65's "reflects the changing dynamics of our population.

Presently, there is a huge debate taking place in our country about how best to fund care for the elderly and appropriate balance between State and private funding as well as the proportion of total costs which should come from differing sources. For this age group, the current range of services and criteria to qualify is utterly confusing leaving literally billions of pounds of unclaimed state benefits. This situation is both inefficient and against the spirit of all policies aimed at financially cushioning our elders against poverty and expediently dispensing state benefits which they have funded and are entitled to.

Possibly, as a society, we might come to resent people living longer, or being kept alive by the wonders of medical science due to the expense and drain on resources involved! I know that this is for most people a harsh and unappetizing proclamation which most certainly alarms and is completely anathema to me. There are many other stark pronouncements contained within this book and I simply want us to all appreciate how some sections of the population may feel when we are weighing up the resources available and how they should be allocated. It is not beyond the bounds of reason that one or more persons in power at some future date and with a substantial following, adopt a view whereby living beyond a certain age becomes financially deleterious whilst some of our elder citizens will live and die in poverty. Be aware that this may not just be what happens in films unless we start debating what to do now.

I seek to highlight an issue many other countries are also grappling with but one facet that I feel passionate about the "**equitable burden of cost**". People currently live for longer and usually require some form of expensive medical and social care compared to even just a decade ago. Care for our senior citizens has to be paid for meaning, as I have mentioned, possible changes are required as to how our finances – public and private are organised. Present day funding modifications should not affect existing people who have reached these pivotal ages and paid for their benefits in taxes and NIC to date. The alterations implemented must relate to the current generation who can better understand and maybe plan for living longer, not those who went through world wars and other conflicts to preserve our way of life and facilitate the current standard of living people enjoy today, especially themselves.

<u>SYNOPSIS</u>

- We should all undertake a **personal audit** acknowledging the faculties that we have and determine what part we can play within the family and society as a whole.

- Happiness underpins the positive elements of life and good health – the key is to determine those factors which lead to our well-being. Seek out which characteristics define each of us and delve into who we really are.

- We can get satisfaction by adopting as far as practical a positive approach to life, being grateful for what we do have and putting the negatives into perspective within our own country and the world as a whole. To me, no one person seems to have it all.

- Within clear parameters persons regardless of their race, colour and ethnic group who have a valid reason to settle in our country must not be debarred from performing their role in society. We must at the same time minimise any scope for unrest amongst those who are indigenous to England.

- Facilitate many others who have the same right as anybody else to function in society to their full capacity without incurring prejudice and barriers such as homosexuals, women, the disabled, young inexperienced people joining the jobs market and people of an advanced age.

- We are not alike and all the better for that. The zealous quest for equality per se is misinformed – Diversity rules.

- Our sex defines us in so many different ways, not least since males cannot bear children.

- Let us applaud **diversity of the sexes** but deplore sexual crimes. No to sexism in the office and as evidence of the side effects relating to this practice refer to the film "*9 to 5*" **a real treat for women, but please do not try this at home or in your workplace!**

- Parents have legal responsibility for their children's actions until aged 18. The age of consent for sex is 16 in England yet the continuing high levels of unwanted pregnancies in young girls is shameful. Holding parents accountable by applying some financial measures against them regarding their sons' and daughters' behaviour, possibly withdrawing state benefits in certain circumstances, should be countenanced to tackle such incidents.

- Nudity in the right place and at the right time please. Sexual matters, lewd and rowdy behaviour in public and sometimes, however, inadvertently in the media and other walks of life, needs to be properly condemned and curtailed. We all have a role to play here.

- Humankind's most precious resources are THE HUMAN ONES. Age must not feature as a major benchmark of suitability for a person's role in society. We can look forward to more octogenarians, nonagenarians and centenarians being with us – **they are part of our history.**

- It is timely to consider if within society we handle our senior citizens in a fitting manner in terms of welfare matters and long-term care provision remembering that **a society is judged by how it deals with the elderly.** We are born as babies, go through our childhood, teenage and adult years, become middle-aged and hope to become advanced in years – this issue matters to us all.

- Financial provision for our elders and the proper split between state and private funding is a huge dilemma in the 21st Century and will continue to be in the future. The apportionment of resources and inevitable increasing costs involved will accompany ever rising longevity rates. We have to sort out the **equitable burden of cost.**

8. COMMUNICATIONS & THE MEDIA IN TODAY'S WORLD

The present era could be known by a variety of titles, the one that springs to my mind most regularly is the **age of information technology (IT).** Pervading and underlying our 24 hour a day lives - computers, laptops, digital cameras and scanning equipment, MP3 media players, e-books, mobile phones, social networking sites such as Facebook and Twitter, e-mail, Web Services such as Paypal, Skype, netbooks, iPads, iPods, iPhones and cloud computing. IT impacts upon almost everything which we think of, say and do. A particular feature of this IT world is just how out of date any information is and so by the time this book is published, there will probably be many more such items.

The media in England has come under the spotlight as never before with the phone hacking scandal whilst internationally via social media like Twitter and Facebook, we have learned first-hand of overseas events like the "Arab spring" of 2011. People have access to information throughout the day and night all year round whilst the motley instruments of surveillance – CCTV, google earth, satellites, mobile phones, wiretapping, have access to us likewise!

ARE WE GETTING THROUGH?

People must control the means of communication, how the media operate and ensure that we understand the data programmed into and data produced by computers which we increasingly rely on. The input and output rests with mankind together with the uses we make of such information. **Science fiction must remain just that, a fantasy and not reality if humans are to survive.**

Evidence comes to light consistently of abuses affecting a person's privacy and entitlement to live and operate under a fair legal system. The UN, the EU and other relevant global institutions must devote time and resources to and then implement regulations extending across international borders and continents for the media and social networks. The transmission of information via computing devices by the protagonists of evil and response by the defenders of our way of life is just as much part of fighting terrorism and wars as other, older mechanisms that we are familiar with. The reality of how IT is employed in such situations is recognised by many of today's leading politicians, business people and those in charge of fighting crime but they are often powerless to act.

The mode by which people are portrayed in the media has a considerable effect on our views towards the world hence those at the top of the hierarchy within media and communication providers have a major responsibility to behave appropriately. Integrity, ethics, accountability and perhaps most importantly the truth must be the dominant factors in their practices. Too many reputations have been ruined, prejudices ingrained in people and false data provided which is deplorable and needs to be addressed for everyone's sake.

More prominence should be afforded to *GOOD NEWS* both at home and abroad. Our demeanour and lives are heavily influenced by what we see, hear and generally absorb noting that we are provided with significantly more bad than good news. Understandably, we obtain a distorted view of events affecting our outlook and decision making. News headlines and editorials frequently deal with a murder, burglary, transport accidents, fires and major disasters all of which are important and should be in the public domain.

Broadcasts should contain less sensationalism like continuing to show footage of the 9/11 atrocities, 7/7 bombings, people rioting in the summer of 2011 etc as a prelude to every time such items are reported on. I firmly believe that we should not have to watch excerpts from surgical operations, injections, dead bodies and other disturbing material on news bulletins, especially during the day and early evenings. Where such matters are covered sometimes a warning is given to the effect that some of the pictures might be disturbing to some people which is fine and appropriate. I refer here to a broader point at issue as to whether repeated lurid footage is not only distressing but when persistently shown, inadvertently helps to desensitise us.

What happens in our country and around the world, good and bad needs to be conveyed to everyone capable of understanding the information provided, not least our young people who must be and usually are aware of events and alive to what people do. There is no suggestion on my part as to shying away from the more shocking features of what is being reported on in accordance with the intended audience. For any facts, statistics and pictures to be continually stated and shown does not always achieve the result required, actually the opposite where people mentally switch off and fail to appreciate the magnitude of what is being reported on.

How about reporting in more detail and as a major news item:-

- Instances of a medical breakthrough that can positively affect millions of people.
- Sporting achievements beneficial to individuals and our country.
- Large trade deals which mean the retention of existing employees and provision of new jobs for hundreds or thousands of people.
- Acts of kindness and charity by people.

These positive, virtuous and pleasant happenings are incorporated within news transmissions and written about in newspapers, but frequently buried in the middle of our news broadcasts and not on the front or back pages of the tabloids and broadsheets alike. I am pleased that many TV news broadcasts have as their final item something positive, light and in fact quite humorous. My plea is for more substantial items to be incorporated within the news programme and so at a more basic level balancing good and evil whilst of course realising that there are occasions where something that happens, at either end of the spectrum inevitably dominates the news and is reported accordingly.

INTERCOURSE OF ALL KINDS

Present day means of communication have demonstrated many benefits which have made a difference to so many lives. Mobile phones via which photographs are taken of somebody or something leading to a police conviction, CCTV's showing a criminal act taking place and helping to identify the miscreant, skype enabling families and friends to share birthday, weddings and such like celebrations in "real time", satellites providing up-to-date and wonderful images across a range of phenomenon anywhere in the world are just a few examples worth mentioning. It is no exaggeration to say that lives are changed forever by dint of communications that would have been unheard of just a couple of decades or even in some instances a few years ago.

I am acutely aware that downsides exist as to how some people talk, write, and generally convey their message to the intended recipients, which concern me and in turn might lead to the loss of other life skills. Our parents and grandparents were confronted by, struggled to cope with and even accept men having long hair, development of what became known as pop (and loud) music, flying in an aeroplane, 24 hour a day TV, cohabitation, homosexuality openly displayed, credit cards not to mention numerous new words as part of our language. We are no different, as the current generation, grappling with what to us seem new fangled and for some, difficult to grasp.

TV Commentators and pundits sometimes employ the use of poor language for example referring in slang to an amount in quid and not pounds or grand not thousands. Over the telephone to any office, commercial undertaking and public service providers an enquiry is sometimes met with responses such as "hold on a minute" or "I don't know", "yeah I think so" and so on. Shortening words or even sometimes using slang is inappropriate in such a situation and offers a poor example to our youngsters as to how they should speak and communicate.

How language is used constitutes much more than me or anybody else being pedantic - it reflects upon a "lack of care and attention to detail" so inherent in much of our communications nowadays. The telephone operator and receptionist used to be the first port of call to a business and showcase their ethos and treatment of customers. Now it is more likely that initial contact will be via email and a website involving less emphasis on the need to demonstrate good use of language and diction but such practices are not only wholly desirable in our business and personal lives but also shows respect for the English language itself.

These examples of how we interact, primarily with regard to younger people mean that too many of this generation have problems with social intercourse. This condition can lead to difficulties in obtaining a job as many employers quite rightly still want people with all round skills including speaking in a proper manner. Our education system also has a vital role to play here seeing that proficient reading and spelling are also often wanting in some school leavers.

Far too much interaction between people amongst some sections of society in these times occurs via swearing, improper body language, the use of knives and other weapons and various forms of aggressive behaviour such as "road rage". One indication of how far society has advanced or not as the case may be, can be illustrated by how many of us email work colleagues in the same building, same office and even sitting next to us in the same office or work space. I recognise and agree that emails are a highly efficient method of proving a record of discussions and meetings, but they seem to be repeatedly used as a substitute for personal contact, a means to avoid the simple exercises like walking and using stairs, exhibiting just plain laziness.

FROM REPUTE TO DISREPUTE

Communications, most notably of more recent origins as referred to above, can be a force for good which has been frequently displayed with many modern day activities that are widely reported in a positive manner. TV Broadcasts, newspapers and social networking sites provide us with information on a variety of events and situations that we would otherwise be unaware of. Some cases in point are:-

- The despicable practices many regimes around the world continue to engage in subjugating their populations.
- The wonderful work that numerous celebrities undertake on behalf of charities.
- Covering major sports events and achievements by many people.
- Uncovering misdemeanours perpetrated by leading businessmen and politicians.
- Highlighting those who work with vulnerable people in society in many different parts of the world.
- Conveying the many campaigns instigated to submit the views of people on a wide range of seeming injustices and policies impacting adversely on a section of society.

I applaud how these activities help to bring about a world where nobody can hide and those who do bad things are more likely to be discovered and hopefully punished accordingly. Most of us have rejoiced at seeing dictators brought down, corrupt politicians removed from their jobs and imprisoned, sports men and women found out via drug tests and banned, religious leaders convicted of sexually abusing children exposed and convicted plus terrorists being caught and brought to book.

Unfortunately, the converse applies all too often where individuals suffer unfairly, witnessing their family life being altered whilst facing bleak futures. The adage which seems so popular with those employed in the media "*what goes up must come down*", is so apt with famous people. Such individuals routinely have their reputations built up to a crescendo if not actually overnight then within a very short timescale, only to endure being denigrated equally quickly with their careers ruined.

In accordance with other themes which I cover in this book, the media collectively have a fiduciary and moral responsibility to *"behave towards others as you would like to have them behave towards you"*. The power of the media has never been greater than in current times, so people who are in the public eye, aspiring artists included, should be mindful of what can happen to their careers, families and lives generally. Many individuals have courted the press and media for their own means including allowing access to their families for what can only be described as "work purposes". Subsequently, when not in their favour and feeling indignant, these same individuals then turn on the media people who they were happy to be interviewed by, complaining to all and sundry at how unfairly they are being treated now. Engage with the media at your own (and sometimes considerable) risk!

Many artists have successfully kept their private lives exactly that "private". I can only try and imagine how difficult this might be, since despite their best intentions, the media can be very intrusive. Presently, as I write these comments, the "phone hacking scandal" has dominated the news together with the actions of the police. In July 2011 the Prime Minister announced a Judicial Inquiry into the role of the press and police in the phone-hacking scandal under Lord Justice Leveson and he published the Leveson Report in November 2012.

I have the utmost respect for those persons who manage to achieve solitude in these circumstances. One name that springs to mind is Gordon Brown (a former Prime Minister) who whatever else he may have been accused of, never allowed the media to photograph or discuss his family whilst in office. There are doubtless many others who preserve as much as possible a private, family life which is to be admired, and as they clearly desire values other than fame and fortune which I feature in this book.

WHOEVER YOU ARE
"THINK FIRST AND SPEAK AFTERWARDS"

Consistently public figures who should know better, make proclamations which they subsequently maintain was either "quoted out of context" "not meant to cause offence" or "said in private". There are in force, quite rightly, strict rules and laws concerning defamation of character, incitement to riot, discrimination of any sort and many other examples of wrongdoing against an individual. I advocate exercising firm control over their vocal chords in front of the media and realise what the responsibilities of their office are together with the effects which their pontifications can have.

The rank and file are outraged, if not totally surprised, when somebody in the public eye utters words which offend people and sometimes sail closely to breaking the moral laws which exist to ban such remarks being made. Diane Abbot, the New Labour MP for Hackney North and Stoke Newington and at the time Shadow Minister for Public Health and David Cameron the UK Prime Minister of the Coalition Government since May 2010 are two such people who have been reported in the media, in recent times, to have made inappropriate comments. They are however, not the only politicians or public figures guilty of making a faux pas which is then widely reported and known through various methods of communication.

I would argue that both of these politicians, and the countless other people who hold positions of authority and via which they have power or influence over our lives, should be severely reprimanded or even contemplated resignation, which they may have done. How difficult it seems to be, and a convoluted process employed by the individual involved, to even say sorry in some form or at least acknowledge the error of their ways. Consider for a moment, how you would be treated, if guilty of issuing form of derisory comment that could impact upon them, by your employer or business colleagues! There must be a suitable price to pay for those occupying lofty, well-paid positions who issue unseemly remarks in my opinion. Eminent people invariably get away with it but should be subject to the same code of conduct and laws which we are all expected to live by.

I accept that somebody who is in the public eye does not have to be a saint or "whiter than white". We all have our foibles and should not incur condemnation or any disproportionate response on every occasion we may err. These persons should know better whether to make such comments at all and the likely impact which they will have but if they must, then do so in private not via any form of public or external form of communication. Unfortunately, there are always people queuing up to exonerate them, something which would not be tolerated if an ordinary person made such utterances. One of my closest friends once told me that *"you cannot unsay what has been said"* how true this is.

Turning now to our national sport - football, unfortunately racial abuse has reared it's ugly head again not in terms of supporters (though no doubt some do still make such remarks), but during the 2011/12 season by Premier League players who are very much in the public eye, perceived as ambassadors for football and the clubs which they play for whilst being handsomely paid for what they do. I am aware that professionals in other sports like cricket, horse racing and athletics have also in recent years in terms of their behaviour disgraced themselves and brought shame to the sport itself.

Luis Suarez a Liverpool Football Club (FC) player from Uruguay and John Terry the Chelsea -FC and at the time this happened also the England national team captain were just two, albeit, the most high profile players embroiled in alleged racial incidents on the pitch itself. Another well-known player at the time from the QPR (Queens Park Rangers) FC, Joey Barton was involved in a violent misconduct charge. In all three cases the players were deemed guilty and punished in the separate cases either by their employer, the Football Association (FA) or both.

Highly paid and revered football players in situations like these quoted (and they are by no means the only ones to be involved in similar instances during this or previous seasons), at this elevated level in the sport take on the mantle of role models to so many people. In particular they serve as examples to young boys and girls playing and watching the game and send out the wrong messages with such disgraceful conduct. Indeed there is evidence that in football matches played by children, teenagers and even adults, such behaviour and outbursts are copied and sometimes accompanied by violence involving spectators, players and even the referee's and their assistants!

I realise that in football like other sports, participants need to be extremely competitive, possess a ruthless streak to win and sometimes, however unwillingly, do act in an unsavoury manner on the spur of the moment. No excuses can be made for how admittedly a minority of sports people react towards their fellow professionals or anybody involved as we all have to exercise self-control at times and more so when millions of TV viewers tune in and whatever you do or say will be reported by the media across the world.

We frequently discover as part of some sort form defence for the culprit about the charity work which they undertake or how outside of the sports arena, they are a different person and not at all like the character they are portrayed to be. Whilst not wishing to diminish the significance of their other activities, individuals who behave badly cannot be absolved of blame on account of what else they do. Many people accused and found guilty of criminal acts are able to demonstrate good character traits which may be instrumental in reducing the severity of any punishments meted out, but does not detract from what they did.

Sport is a massive pastime for countless people and nowadays there is so much coverage that is live on TV and accessible on various gadgets referred at the outset of this section. Some footballers and such like at the top of their game are now megastars and celebrities in their own right, largely on account of the money swishing around and with major sports now such big business. We do not expect our heroes to be squeaky-clean but have a right to at least watch them operating within certain bounds of decency. Today, however, fame and wealth unimaginable to most supporters has largely ruined the kernel of some sports, especially football, so the attendant pressure to perform and achieve results to a large extent explains how sports are organised, managed and played.

There is no place in our lives for potentially inflammatory and insulting behaviour or actions and this must equally apply to the better known figures in society. Failing to be contrite is highly damaging to their roles in society and themselves individually, but most telling is unacceptable in any sphere be it sports, politics, business, entertainment or everyday life generally.

From your standpoint, how should those at the top of their profession behave whilst engaged in their sport and generally what, if any, are their responsibilities to fans, the club which employs and pays them together with the wider public.

JARGON AND MODERN SPEAK

For a moment consider these familiar phrases in vogue today (although they are not all new):-

- Driving forwards.
- Taking a hit across the range of.....
- Stakeholders in the community.
- Reviewing all of our systems and controls.
- We can add value.
- Our customers (not patients or members).
- Foot flow (through banks, shops and other establishments).
- Escalate your enquiry.
- Turnaround teams.
- Debt rescheduling.

K.I.S.S. as stated in the section on the economy and finance should prevail more. Reduce jargon, let us have fewer "isms" and buzz words, gobbledygook, and management speak. Anybody, especially politicians and industry leaders can and customarily do, say vague, puerile statements like:-

- We promise to.........
- We are working towards...............
- All of our stakeholders.

- We are totally focused on……….
- We are fully committed to solving this issue.
- This must not be allowed to happen again.
- Our systems and procedures are robust.

Maybe there are sayings or phrases that are irksome to you – get them off your chest here

Continuing with this theme, I maintain that we are increasingly becoming accustomed to a description of people's job s which seems either designed to obscure what they do or take in a variety of functions. I do not like the term Government "**czars/tsars"** which I feel is inappropriate implying a supreme ruler or emperor for a particular field or industry! Those deemed to hold have held this position in history were generally looked upon with distaste and I fail to see why we want to call anybody today by this title.

In my opinion, there is a trend towards obfuscating how some businesses operates, what a person's job entails and inventing a whole new terminology for today. Naturally, as throughout history, we need to keep up with developments in the world and changes to our way of life where in many cases, a word or expression rapidly becomes mainstream and part of our everyday vocabulary. New jargon and terminology is often needed to describe or explain what something is or how it operates. We must guard against using pointless language which might only serve to artificially justify somebody's actual role in a firm or political party as well as their remuneration.

The acid test is whether a **reasonably educated person** comprehends within a few minutes of listening to or reading about any given situation, what is involved. A term well-known now to describe how a person might be expressing themselves is to "blind somebody with science". The English language is rich with words to use and most people, unless they are avid readers across all genres of literature, are only familiar with a tiny part of what is contained within a modern dictionary or thesaurus. In the company of others, be prepared to politely challenge somebody to explain the meaning of a particular term, phrase or expression.

Many politicians and captains of industry have their speeches written for them, and it is the speech writers more often than not, who like to invent some new turn of phrase. There are occasions during such an address when we glean a highly appropriate, modern way of articulating a particular state of affairs. Too often, however, the opposite applies and we are left wondering what it was all about. One of the greatest compliments my younger son has paid me in the past is a description as "modern man" in terms of how I communicate, dress (sometimes) as well as my musical and film tastes. Contemporary use of language is a logical feature of society as it progresses, but let us ensure that it is fitting and user-friendly.

<u>SYNOPSIS</u>

- We live in an **age of information technology (IT)**, as evidenced by the various appliances on the market and which many people own. Our lifestyles also reflect this situation and we never seem to be turned off!

- Human beings must hold sway over the means of communication available, the functioning of the media in all of it's guises and how information is managed – **science fiction must remain just that, a fantasy and not reality if humans are to survive.**

- People working in the media must act more responsibly and recognise everyone's right to privacy. News disseminated should be balanced between what is good and bad and for the latter, maybe less explicit footage repeatedly shown will have a better effect on viewers.

- Like all developments to date, modern methods of communication offers us advantages and disadvantages – invariably nothing is all good or all bad. The language which we use says much about a person and society as a whole.

- One notable detrimental facet regarding the transmission of information by the media is the apparent obsession with putting famous people and rising starlets on a pedestal, only to then delight in taking them down again. I exhort those who are culpable to consider the adage **behave towards others as you would like to have them behave towards you.**

- Well-known figures and people in the public eye need to think it all over before saying anything and accept the consequences where these cause offence and have an adverse impact on others.

- Professionals at the top of their sports in particular football, plus those who are influential in other areas of our life such as politics, business matters and the entertainment industry must guard against sending out the wrong messages and consider how they portray themselves.

- Our understanding of much information produced today would be significantly improved where people utilize jargon and phrases particular to their spheres, sparingly, in the right context and to the right audience.

- Some individuals have job descriptions that are vague and even defy any understanding. High-ranking politicians and senior business people often deliver speeches written for them which include expressions and words that make little sense to listeners.

- The litmus test for communications is whether a **reasonably educated person** can understand within a few minutes what they are listening to or reading about.

POSTSCRIPT – IT's YOUR CALL

Well you have reached the end of this whirlwind tour of my mind amounting to personal reflections on what is happening to us at the start of the second decade of the 21st Century and I expect that there are many thoughts and ideas floating around in your mind. These pages cannot do justice to the wide compass of topics referred to or the many talking points which feasibly have emerged. Perhaps you vehemently disagree with some of the conclusions reached, had not considered some of the issues in the particular light set out here and maybe even see eye to eye with me on occasions.

The book is intended as a forum for deliberation, solutions to be considered and action to be taken by all who feel able to do so. Hopefully, you now feel either animated, aggravated, astounded or all three of these emotions! Undoubtedly, you can provide some feedback which I urge you to do whilst the book's contents are fresh in your mind. Conceivably, the information which you submit in conjunction with that of other readers who do likewise might result in the creation and implementation of an outline programme of action over time.

Too often we simmer internally without appreciating that our friends, family, work colleagues in fact a whole host of people all around us have similar feelings and an inclination to do something about matters. I implore you not to be reticent and perhaps take that important first step by making up your mind to react. This publication should act as a fulcrum for what happens next and it is up to you.

I harbour no illusion that one book, whoever the author is and however popular it may become, will achieve the elixir of instant happiness and solve all or even a minority of today's perceived problems. Numerous eminent philosophers, historians, religious leaders, economists, politicians, business magnates, medical professors, experts on the social sciences and successful sports people have made valuable contributions to all aspects of our lives, documenting their trials and tribulations and providing excellent insights into their particular specialist field and the wider world. Specialist's articles have shed light on and helped us towards finding the key to a few of the issues which I have majored on in the preceding pages. Many intractable problems, however, still remain.

Perchance, humanity will always be confronted with difficulties and stumbling blocks so it is fanciful of me to suggest that we can ever solve all the problems that emerge let alone reach some kind of nirvana. Plausibly there are defects inherent in us and so each generation has to deal as best they can with whatever issues arise at the time and, moreover, this is how people learn, invent new ideas and move on. Wars, epidemics, the desire to explore here on earth and in space, natural disasters and such like spur people on to understand these phenomena and undertake improvements to our lifestyles. My lofty ambition may not be achievable, but how much worse off humanity would be if people stopped expressing their aspirations.

The book is predicated on even a handful of individuals thinking of and being prepared to make an effort towards establishing a different basis for our existence and tackling these problems. One outcome which I would be pleased about, is for you to be one of those individuals who is stimulated by some of the material and ideas put forward in the preceding pages to react and start the ball rolling.

I am convinced that latent desires to change matters exist amongst some of you who are reading this book and possess the talent to move us all forward to the next level. I have no claim to any particular successes in life to date neither am I endowed with any specialist attributes in order to found and lead a political party, movement or crusade so instigating a whole new model of life. I sincerely wish to tap into those individuals who are suited to this task and consider that some of this book's subject matter serves as a foundation for such a project. Any tangible results along these lines might take years before coming to light but a start needs to be made now.

We have been subject to a multitude of cosmetic changes to the outer layers of society in recent times some of which have accomplished limited success. In the main, however, these have plastered over the cracks and not impinged on the fabric itself. Previously tried and failed government policies are wheeled out in some new guise, PC has reached a new level of absurdity hampering genuine ideas being put forward and action taken for fear of causing offence to anybody. In many cases, what are deemed to be old-fashioned concepts become discarded, authority in assorted areas like law and order, education and parenting has all but broken down completely whilst money, short-termism and external appearances seem to hold sway.

The gap in terms of earnings between those at the top of the pile and nearer to the bottom in employment structures has expanded in recent decades, children are failing to receive the education required to gain jobs in the workplace, respect has to be promoted as against being part of our ethics and moral code of behaviour whilst many forms of criminal activity continue unabated. Despite the availability of healthier foods plus campaigns alerting people to the dangers involved, obesity is rising, alarmingly amongst the youngest age group, which along with other self-inflicted disorders emanating from drug taking and alcohol consumption divert precious healthcare resources away from other, and some would maintain, more deserving causes. I wish to reaffirm that not all instances of obesity and the excessive use of drugs and alcohol are the fault exclusively of the individual involved accepting that there can be other elements at play.

In trying to flesh out people who are able and willing to endorse the need for a whole new framework covering our lives, I wholeheartedly embrace the promising developments observed in recent times but we must not be complacent. We generally live much longer than in previous ages, enjoy the use of public resources taken for granted like clean water, energy and waste disposal whilst the cost of various modes of transport enable us to visit and appreciate the merits of many locations in our own country and the wider world. The internet has truly revolutionised our whole existence with many more benefits than weaknesses. Other aspects of technology constantly move us nearer to what could be only science fiction during our parent's childhood, or even our own!

In particular we must all welcome the disappearance of many killer diseases from our shores that decimated children as well as adults even into the beginning of the 20th Century. The arrival of the Space Age in the 1950's shed new light on our planet, moon, sun and the whole universe. We have also witnessed improved methods of contraception as well as an understanding of and means to help with infertility. Many people now own and wear a wide range of clothing, a relatively high level of home ownership applies whilst people can enjoy a huge selection of leisure activities. Across the board, people have a vastly improved perspective on women, disabled people and the elderly compared to previous epochs – much more still needs to be done for these folk.

There is up-to-date information about almost anything that we could want or need at our fingertips together with a full ambit of goods and services normally available within price ranges affordable to most people all unimaginable when I was a child. An increasing percentage of the world's population live under democratically elected governments and thankfully there are now fewer people having to endure dictatorial and brutal political regimes – still too many for comfort.

In England there is an increasing amount of evidence for a resurgence of interest in religion with demand for more faith schools for our children and people becoming more spiritual as they realise that materialism and monetary wealth are not the basis for a happy life. Various political and other initiatives launched in recent times have centred on communal activities and participation in local and regional events. I commend those wealthy and famous people from the world of entertainment (and many other fields) who have decided to use their star appeal for spearheading wonderful projects in parts of the world where still far too many underprivileged people live in deplorable conditions and infant mortality is at stubbornly high levels.

The human race (with some exceptions) has belatedly recognised that our planet's resources are in some cases finite and have to be allocated more efficiently than in the past. We are also much more aware as to the desirability of protecting the environment even in comparison with the later decades of the 20th Century. This new perspective is now evidenced by how our political leaders are trying to put the brakes on various developments, whilst industrial giants can no longer just ruthlessly pursue an agenda without taking account of environmental considerations (at least in theory). Living as we do in a progressive age can also be derived from a wholly justifiably more enlightened approach taken towards sexual matters, other people's cultures.

I resolutely believe that people from all walks of life are inclined towards a novel approach to the plight that we are all in as discussed in the aforementioned pages. In the realms of - debt reduction, breakdown in law and order, appropriate welfare provision, the machinations of our political system, power of the media, unemployment and disengagement of countless young people from mainstream society, short-term goals pursued in the fields of politics and business together with the impact of increasing longevity on society in line with financial provision for the elderly - we must reappraise all of the systems in place and their effectiveness.

I would propound that - potholes need mending, streets should be kept clean, police ought to be visible on our main streets in town and city centres, hospitals have to be LOCAL whilst municipal parks should be tidy and patrolled to be safe and inviting for everyone to benefit all patrons. Furthermore, all unsuitable material for children and adolescents must be screened after a watershed time, governments should cease their insatiable appetite for borrowing amounts that cannot realistically be paid back – all of these would help us to get underway in the quest for basic improvements sorely needed. Returning to sensible parameters within which the media can operate, taking measures so that confidence can be speedily restored in political leaders and business people who are in the public eye together with the need for talking in straightforward terms and ensuring that everyone is accountable for their actions and utterances where they are not suffering from any medical impediment and deemed sane will also contribute to a renaissance of a **common sense society.**

Prompt fixing and repairs of water pipes and such like would help reduce leakages and the need to impose drought orders and raise water charges in a country which on average does normally receive a lot of rainfall each year, measured over say a decade. Aligned with water usage and rainfalls, we could ensure that especially in Autumn, leaves are regularly swept away as they often block drains.

I also venture to suggest that incorporated within the essence of principles and standards that we live by, the instances of promiscuity and lewd behaviour amongst some sections of society should be more frowned upon than it is now.   Respect for people has to be earned by as well as given to them. Maybe products that we buy can be retained for longer as against being replaced when a part ceases to function or they are considered to be "out of date" and "old-fashioned".

We can also aspire to save a proportion of our earnings for the future, in particular to fund for retirement as people now expect to live well into their 80's and even 90's. Clearly the age of "state provision" and even "fully or partially employer financed pension schemes" is well and truly over.

A CULTURE OF SAVINGS
LEADS TO

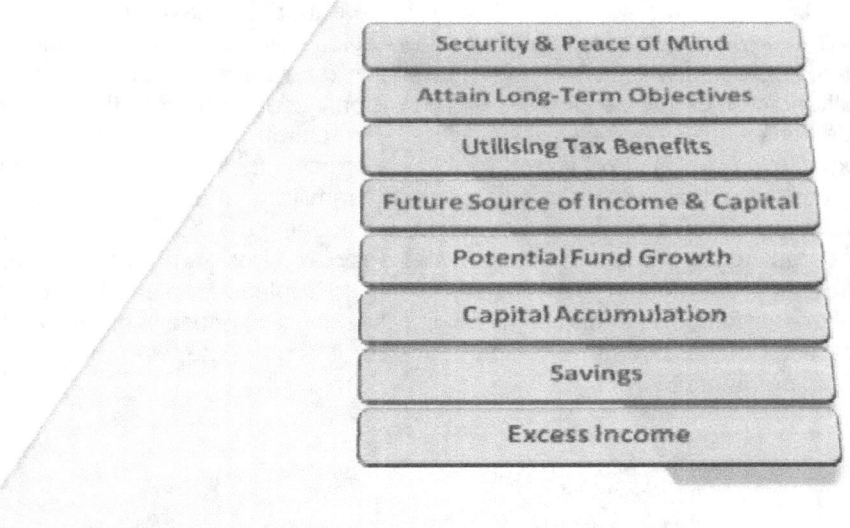

Security & Peace of Mind

Attain Long-Term Objectives

Utilising Tax Benefits

Future Source of Income & Capital

Potential Fund Growth

Capital Accumulation

Savings

Excess Income

We must be realistic as to what can be achieved but this should not detract from making a start.

Perhaps the good people of England need to stand up and demonstrate (peacefully) more to express their points of view, start up and run campaigns against injustices using all available forms of media (which has occurred more of late) and learn to say NO whilst seeking to control and influence our own destiny. Learning of and embracing practices and customs emanating from people in other parts of the world is highly beneficial where they are suited to the citizens and way of life in England.

The world is becoming smaller by the day but paradoxically, people increasingly want to be associated with their own kind whether in terms of ethnicity, religious groupings, local amenities and laws but generally smaller, more accountable and comprehensible units. Folk across the world feel progressively detached from the global economy, international institutions, sweeping laws governing people's way of life and far-reaching changes affecting each person's locale. Here at home, David Cameron keeps banging on about the BIG SOCIETY, but what so many people clearly want and need is the "small society" with more localism.

Mere mortals cannot always cope with the pace of change happening today and all-pervasive nature of phenomenon. Indeed, some instances come to mind where change needs to happen, if at all, at a much slower pace for the people involved to remotely understand and accept what is involved. Change needs to be for the local inhabitant's interests predominantly, or at least equally for their benefit, when emanating externally.

There is a tendency for some individuals in power today in parts of the world, such as the so-called West, to believe that they have duty to impose their lifestyle on people inhabiting other regions on our planet. I refer here to democracies which by taking such action (sometimes in association with military force), may be ignoring, or paying only scant regard to their wishes, traditions and way of life. In practice, the regime to put in place on that region's inhabitants is different to what is normal in their territory. Individuals across the globe want to associate with the familiar and existing conventions to underpin their lives, but this does not mean being closed to new concepts, undertakings or means of subsistence. Probably along with many people I shudder at the thought of somebody coming to England from another country, culture or following a particular religion seeking to impose their views and practices on us, but some people consider it appropriate, even our duty, to do so on others!

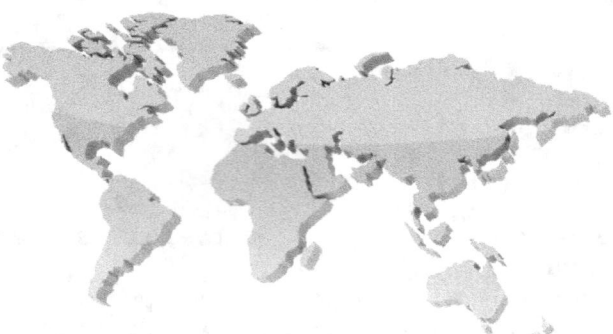

Like so many others, I detest how some regimes operate in various locations around the world which of course we are now aware of and are more difficult to keep hidden by dint of modern, speedy means of communication that we now have. In the past, fascism, communism and a whole host of political movements have inevitably failed and eventually the wishes of the people are met, but only after much death and suffering by innocent civilians. We must, however, be mindful of what authority any country and it's political leaders possess to initiate changes elsewhere and if we do, whether there is consistency in the approach to all regimes that are considered to be ripe for bringing down.

We cannot turn the clock back and going back in time should continue to be in the realms of science fiction (and spawn many more good films in the process). Continually zeroing into the past is counterproductive since mankind must move forward as it always has done but we can and should analyse history to avoid repeating the mistakes already made. By the same token, we can lament, as I do, moving away from many values that characterised preceding eras and even the recent past that would hold as good today as before.

I perceive much that is good in our world today, with lots to be thankful for and are convinced that some lessons from the past have been well and truly learned. Undeniably, our lives are more enlightened in so many ways compared to even the more recent past, which I fully acknowledge. With the right people coming forth who have the capability, desire and most importantly determination to propel us onwards, some form of new or revised **platform for life** can evolve over time and humanity can realise a true **shift in paradigm.**

MY APPRECIATION OF OTHER PEOPLE INVOLVED

I have realised during the research undertaken, drafting up of the subject matter and finalising the book's contents that a multitude of people have been involved and are entitled to share in the credit for this venture which now sees the light of day. Truly indeed *"No man is an island"*.

My eldest son sowed the seeds for the book by his suggestion of using the time which I now have due to my effective early retirement on account of ill-health for writing a book about the wisdom which he considered I have as somebody in my 50's. He said to relate my experiences, thoughts and general observations on life which is exactly what I have endeavoured to do. My thanks to him for this proposition which has led me to do something that I have really enjoyed and hopefully will interest and benefit many other people.

My youngest son has a knack in selecting as a present exactly the right books for my birthday as he is very attentive concerning my activities and interests. For a recent birthday after my first forays into writing some text were mooted, he bought a book on creative writing which was of enormous help to me as a virgin author so I am very grateful to him for this inspired purchase. I have, of course, referred to various other publications for information and were surprised to discover how useful some of the books which have resided in our house for decades (and I was not familiar with) including those representing prizes at school received by my wife, actually were.

Regularly attending the local synagogue that my family are members of, I am always keen to hear the Rabbi's weekly sermon which lasts on average for 15-20 minutes, noticing those congregants who fall asleep or from their facial expressions are clearly thinking of other matters! In particular, quite a few of these spiritual leaders have influenced me by the way that they have interwoven secular and religious issues and demonstrated a keen insight into and recognition of the problems humankind face today.

At various social gatherings with family and friends, I have been encouraged when the subject of this book surfaced in conversation, by just how enthusiastic their reaction has been. Their views and comments on some of the subject matter brought to me a realisation of how extensively people around me, and no doubt numerous others, feel despondent, ignored, let down and generally powerless to act and influence events. The input of people who I trust and know very well at these get-togethers spurred me on even more to ensure that this endeavour came to fruition.

My wife in addition to fulfilling the roles of being a true soul mate to me and best friend for over three decades, has endured my regular outbursts when some form of literary epiphany came to me and overall zeal with which I have pursued this writing activity over the past couple of years. She frequently read over the contents making a valuable contribution to the layout, together with the excellent graphics used throughout the book. A consummate secretary who amongst other posts worked with me as a personal assistant for over 14 years, she has grasped the new technology much better than myself which in conjunction with her aptitude for visuals in order to make a point, hopefully enhances the book. I am delighted that the graphics contained within the book enables readers to consider some issues from a pictorial standpoint. It is impossible to properly express in just a few words, how supportive she has been and the part played in the appearance of this book.

Like everyone who has lost a loved one I miss my parents, who both died within the last few years enormously, and think of them in some way every single day. My father (may he rest in peace), was the person who probably had the most impact on my life, a truly wise man able to articulate himself on almost any issue, feel comfortable engaging with a whole cross-section of people and together with my mother, instilled in me true family values. My whole approach to writing in the manner which I have, and whatever wisdom I possess that has found it's way into this book, largely derives from my father's influence and I am proud to document my gratitude to him.

Ultimately, I thank you for acquiring a copy of this book and investing time to read the contents which I hope proved to be enjoyable and productive. There is an ever increasing range and amount of books available covering every conceivable topic making it all the more important to me that you have chosen to read this one.

Thank you everyone, I am indebted to you all who have played a part in the book and may we all witness **A Shift In Paradigm.**

NOTES:-

Page 36 - Answer

£1 billion = 1 thousand millions   (1 & 9 zeros)
1,000,000,000 or 10^9

£1 trillion = 1 thousand billions   (1 & 12 zeros)
1,000,000,000,000 or 10^{12}

Page 47 – 48 - Answer

1)	**18**	8)	**16**
2)	**18**	9)	**17**
3)	**16**	10)	**14**
4)	**18**	11)	**17**
5)	**16**	12)	**5**
6)	**10**	13)	**13**
7)	**16**	14)	**15**

For your feedback and comments please email the author at
info@jdmilaric.com

REFERENCES

Time waits for no man - Origin of this ancient phrase is uncertain, although it predates modern English. The earliest known record is from St. Marher, 1225 and a version of this in modern English is "the tide abides for, tarrieth for no man, stays no man, tide nor time tarrieth no man" and it appears that this evolved into the phrase we use today. Also associated with the fable King Canute of Denmark. Essentially is the notion of "tide" being beyond man's control.

History repeats itself - Karl Marx the German Philosopher and revolutionary (1818-1883) said in "The Eighteenth Brumaire of Louis Bonaparte (1852) "Hegel remarks somewhere that history tends to repeat itself. He forgot to add: the first time as a tragedy, the second time as farce"

Sitting on the fence - David Lloyd George (1863-1945) the British Prime Minister (1916 – 1922) and Liberal Statesman quoted with reference to Sir John Simon "The Right Honourable gentleman has sat for so long on the fence that the iron has entered into his soul".

The love of money is the root of all evil - Proverb – biblical quote original source is the Book of Timothy 6:10 (King James version).

Keeping up with the Joneses - Phrase invented by the cartoonist Arthur R. Momand for a comic-strip series which began in the New York Globe on 1st April 1913

We don't throw the baby out with the bathwater - Emanates from German. First known appearance in English from Scottish historian and political philosopher Thomas Carlyle who wrote in 1853 "The Germans say, You must empty out the bathing-tub, but not the baby along with it".

Mission Statement – American in origin and first taken up by the British in the early 1990's.

There are three kinds of lies: lies, damned lies and statistics - Benjamin Disraeli the 1st Earl of Beaconsfield (1804 – 1881).

NEET (Not in Employment, Education or Training) - Government acronym first used in the UK in a 1999 SEU (Social Exclusion Unit) report.

Fit For Purpose - Means being good enough to do the job it was designed to do. European Law dictates that goods must be fit for purpose. Labour Home Secretary John (now Lord) Reid was reported to have quoted this to the

Immigration and Nationality Directorate in 2006 but has since clarified that it was actually said by a senior civil servant, and not himself.

K.I.S.S. (Keep it Simple, Stupid) - Acronym which is well-known within sales and deemed as a very successful sales tactic.

Economical with the truth - Euphemism for being untruthful, issued by the Cabinet Secretary Sir Robert Armstrong, to the Supreme Court, New South Wales, Australia in the Spycatcher Trial. Referring to a letter Sir Robert said "It contains a misleading impression, not a lie. It was being economical with the truth" (reported in the Daily Telegraph 19th November 1986)

Buck stops here - US President Harry S Truman had this as the wording of a sign on his desk in the Oval Office indicating that the ultimate responsibility for running the country lay with him. Expression dates from the 1940's alluding to the 19th Century phrase "to pass the buck" meaning evade blame or responsibility or shift it onto someone else.

It takes two to tango - The title of a song written in 1952 "Takes Two to Tango" by Al Hoffman and Dick Manning. In Latin tango means "I touch" and the tango is usually regarded as a sexually charged South American dance

Sign of the times - A phrase strongly associated with Roman Catholicism in the era of the Second Vatican Council (1962 – 1965). It was taken to mean that the church should listen to and learn from, the world around it
England is a nation of shopkeepers - Disparaging remark used by Napoleon I to describe the UK as unfit for war against France. Actually originates with the famous Scottish Economist – Adam Smith in his book "An Inquiry into the Nature and Causes of the Wealth of Nations".

Prevention is better than cure - Written by the Dutch Humanist and Scholar Erasmus Desiderius (1466-1536). Also the US Scientist and Statesman Benjamin Franklin (1706-1790) said in 1736 "An ounce of prevention is better than a pound of curse".

Food for thought - Meaning that something deserves serious consideration and has been in the language since the early 19th Century

You are what you eat - The phrase emerged in English in the 1920's and 1930's. The Nutritionist Victor Lindlahr developed a specific diet and in an advert for beef in a 1923 edition of the Bridgeport Telegraph for "United Meet (sic) Markets" he said "Ninety per cent of the diseases known to man are caused by cheap foodstuffs and You are what you eat"

Mind your Ps and Q's - English expression meaning to mind your manners and be on your best behaviour, be careful to avoid giving offence. Has been known since the 17th Century but the exact origins are uncertain

Binge drinking - A book from 1854 called "A Glossary of Northamptonshire" had recorded "A man goes to the alehouse to get a good binge, or to binge himself".   Generally considered to be a modern problem, but people have always drunk to excess.

Power corrupts and absolute power corrupts absolutely - This was an opinion expressed by a British Historian and Moralist - John Dalberg, 1st Baron of Acton (1834-1902) in a letter of 3rd April 1887 to Bishop Mandell Creighton which said "Power tends to corrupt, and absolute power corrupts absolutely. Great men are almost always bad me, even when they exercise influence and not authority".

Political Correctness (PC) - The concept originated in the USA during the 1980's as a term for the avoidance of words or actions that are perceived to insult disadvantaged groups. PC is recorded in 1840 in the USA and in 1793 the US Supreme Court records refers to the term political correct. Originally these terms referred to people conforming to the prevailing political views of the time.

Pass the buck - Means to shift responsibility to someone else or evade blame. To pass the buck is to hand over responsibility for dealing the cards to the next player.

Twenty-four-seven - Meaning every day, all of the time, around the clock. The expression dates from the 1980's and was coined in America as back street slang.

Order out of chaos - Latin phrase "ordo ab chao" and one of the oldest mottoes of the Ancient Craft Masonry (1395)

Do not be afraid - Deuteronomy 31.8 "The Lord himself goes before you and will be with you; he will never leave you nor forsake you: Do not be afraid; do not be discouraged".

Straight and narrow - Generally means the honest and morally acceptable way of living and also to stay out of trouble. The earliest reference is the King James Version of the bible, Matthew 7:13/14 "Because strait is the gate, and narrow is the way which leadeth unto life, and few there be that find it". A more recent reference is in John Bunyan's book "The Pilgrim's Progress" published in 1678. In it, Pilgrim, the representative of the Everyman, must follow the "straight & narrow"

Three score years and ten - Three score is an old-fashioned way of saying age 60. According to Psalm 90 from the bible (King James Version) "The days of our age are threescore years and ten"

A society is judged by how it deals with the elderly - The US Novelist – Pearl S Buck (1892-1973) wrote in "My Several Worlds" (1954) "our society must make it right and possible for old people not to fear the young or be deserted by them for the test of a civilization is the way that it cares for its helpless members"

Behave towards others as you would like to have them behave towards you – The so called "Golden Rule" also known as the "ethic of reciprocity" is stated in almost all forms of ancient writing (Talmud, New Testament, Koran and many of the world's major religions) about behavioural concepts. The Jewish Sage – Hillel (110BCE-10CE) when asked to sum up the entire Torah concisely answered "That which is hateful to you, do not do to your fellow. That is the entire Torah; the rest is the explanation; go and learn" (Talmud, Shabbat 31a)

Think first and speak afterwards - Various origins are cited for this proverb, some of which are biblical (New Testament). Jean de la Bruyere a French Satirist (1645-1696) said "There are some who speak one moment before they think".

No man is an island - John Donne and English Poet and Preacher (1573-1631) wrote in "Devotions Upon Emergent Occasions" (1624) "No man is an Island, entire of itself; every man is a piece of the continent, a part of the main".